NICE TIMING

GOURMET MEALS IN MINUTES

NICE TIMING

GOURMET MEALS IN MINUTES

Pamela Steel

Based on the column from *President's Choice® Magazine*

Prentice Hall Canada

A Pearson Company
Toronto

Canadian Cataloguing in Publication Data

Steel, Pamela
Nice timing: gourmet meals in minutes

Includes index.

ISBN 0-13-018185-4

1. Quick and easy cookery. 2. Menus I. Title
TX833.5.S73 2000 641.5'55 C00-930124-0

ISBN 0-13-018185-4

Editorial Director, Trade Division: Andrea Crozier
Acquisitions Editor: Nicole de Montbrun
Copy Editor: Madeline Koch
Production Editor: Jodi Lewchuk
Art Direction: Mary Opper
Cover Design and Interior Design: Tania Craan
Cover Photographs: Robert Fiocca (Front Cover: Frogmore Stew, p. 172; Mango and Avacado Salad, p.8; Squash and Apple Soup with Crème Fraîche, p. 120. Back Cover: Nori-Wrapped Chicken, p. 40; Raspberry White Chocolate Puffs, p.24.)
Interior Photographs: 1, 3, 6, 7, 8, Michael Kohn; 2, 4, 5, Robert Fiocca
Production Manager: Kathrine Pummell
Page Layout: Kyle Gell

1 2 3 4 5 KR 04 03 02 01 00

Printed and bound in Canada.

Prentice Hall Canada

A Pearson Company

For Bill, my husband and partner in everything.

Contents

Acknowledgments

As always, I would accomplish nothing without the support, the help, the guidance and the amazing culinary skills of my husband, Bill. He was instrumental in the writing of this book, from choosing and inventing recipes to running my test kitchen to doing the first copy edit. Thanks to my son, Nathan, whose light is the great happiness of my life.

The column would never had gotten off the ground without the support of Patricia Holtz, the editor of *President's Choice® Magazine.* Pat has been a guiding force throughout this project and working with her has always been a joy. Many thanks to Sasha Chapman, Senior Food Editor at *President's Choice® Magazine,* who does a terrific job at crossing my Ts, dotting my Is and making sure I put eggs in my soufflés. With the rest of their team, Pat and Sasha have put together a world-class magazine celebrating Canadian cuisine that I am pleased and proud to be a part of. For making me look good, I am eternally grateful to Carol Moskot, the magazine's art director, and Erika Oliveira, Associate Art Director. Special thanks to all the great photographers who do such stunning visual work, especially Rob Fiocca and Michael Kohn, whose photographs appear in this book. Thanks to the many food stylists who lend their talents to the look of the column, and to Jenny Koniuk, the recipe tester who cooks every meal and whose invaluable opinion is always appreciated. A very special thanks to the readers of *President's Choice® Magazine,* for picking us up every month—without you, we're nothing,

A world of thanks to my friend and editor at Prentice Hall, Nicole de Montbrun, who has been an advocate of my work since the very beginning. And thanks to Prentice Hall's editorial director Andrea Crozier, production editor Jodi Lewchuk, copy editor Madeline Koch, art director Mary Opper, designer Tania Craan, production manager Kathrine Pummell and formatter Kyle Gell.

Thanks to Catherine (The Grape) Lashko for sharing her extensive wine knowledge. Special thanks to every cook, chef and pastry chef I have ever had the privilege of working with; every one of you has taught me something. Most notably to the late André Théberge, whose recipes and style continually pop up in my work, and to Elie Benchitrit of Provence Restaurant. To Frank Scordino, Executive Chef at the Senator restaurant, whose busy schedule doesn't stop him from lending his excellent advice, and to Stefanie Killen for her great ideas in the pastry department. And, as always, thanks to Trisse Loxely for getting the ball rolling.

For All Seasons

With cooking, as in life, timing is everything. In a second, caramel turns from delightfully sweet to bitter and burned. A cake taken from the oven too soon is a disappointment in many ways. Orchestrating a dinner, like an opera, is a matter of talent, grace and precision timing. All the elements of the successful production must be brought together at just the right moment to create the final masterpiece. As a professional chef, I have perfected many tricks and strategies for pulling together the event that is a wonderful meal, and I am pleased to pass them on to you in this book.

Of course, you are not working in a restaurant kitchen, preparing and organizing the fine details of a hundred dinners. You have spent the day at your profession and now are interested in putting dinner on the table with as little fuss as possible. But does lack of time and energy mean the evening's repast need be pedestrian and dull? Are we condemned to a life of frozen foods and convenience quickies? And would this life really be worth living? The menus in this book are testament to the fact that cooking elegant food is still an option for the time-pressed cook. Give me one hour and I will give you a meal fit to be savoured. Certainly there are days when even an hour is more than can be afforded, but for those times when the sanctuary of your kitchen is a welcome relief and a three-course dinner would be a happy balm for your tired spirit, then a little *Nice Timing* is for you.

Purists will scoff at dishes like Chicken Mole and, indeed, such a recipe is meant to be cooked over days, not minutes. However, with some tinkering, I have managed to simplify this and many other classics with excellent results. This simplification also means that the more novice cook can attempt dishes that might otherwise be inaccessible. In these pages lie methods for the most demystified chocclate soufflé, coq au vin and pots-du-crème imaginable. Some of the finer points have been shaved off and the dishes streamlined but the end product retains the essence of the original, with all the flavour and enough of the finesse to impress.

Some of these columns have already appeared in *President's Choice® Magazine,* where *Nice Timing* appears as a monthly column. It has been exciting over the last two years to hear from readers who regularly use *Nice Timing* as a guide for preparing meals at home. They have been generous with their praise and I am thrilled that so many people have enjoyed cooking and, most importantly, eating the meals that I have designed. I am certain that part of its popularity is due to the fact that the recipes are tested first by me (repeatedly), then by my editor and the team of food stylists and recipe testers. These food professionals guarantee that the magazine's recipes will work in your home kitchen.

As a part of every column, I include a wine suggestion to accompany each meal. I first began my study of the grape while working at Raclette Restaurant in Toronto under the tutelage of Sebastien Van Merendonk. Sebastien had a great deal of knowledge to share, and another avid pupil was the restaurant's manager, Catherine Lashko. Catherine has gone on to become the Director of Food and Beverage for the elegant Windsor Arms Hotel and is now one short essay away from obtaining her sommelier's papers. Several of the menus in the book benefit from her extensive wine knowledge.

I write this just before Christmas in the year 1999. There is speculation that the world will be profoundly changed as the clock ticks and we emerge over the rim of morning in the early minutes of the year 2K. If you are reading this, then we have all come out just fine and are still interested in the entertainment and edification of cookbooks. Excellent.

S P R I N G

A breeze was coming through the hole in the kitchen wall,
and it felt almost mild. I could hear something dripping.
When I went outside, I found that the seasons had changed.
The stone table was oozing water, and spring had arrived.

–*Peter Mayle,* A Year in Provence

Come March 1, I invest my menus with a splash of colour or a hint of fancy to lighten my spirits. Spring lamb and tiramisu lift me up and soothe my winter-weary heart. For a meal with a more tropical breeze, I offer coconut curried shrimp, mango and avocado salad, and sorbet with rum sauce. In like a lamb and out like a lambada dancer. April showers bring May showers: signs that very soon we'll be able to feast on foods from our own soil. Vegetarian cuisine makes a good showing in a menu built on Zucchini Parmigiana and a spinach gnocchi that is, without a doubt, my favourite dish in this book, next to chocolate. And speaking of chocolate, since I began cooking and writing about it, I've gained 10 pounds a year because I spend too much time perfecting each recipe (I made 12 versions of the Chocolate Bourbon Pots-du-Crème on page 20!). The late spring "spa" menus that follow are good for my heart in more ways than one. When preparing these menus, I veer toward fish, vegetables, fruits and a virtually fat-free angel food cake.

MENU FOR TWO

Lamb Loins and Sauce

Mixed Greens with Chèvre

Herbed Vegetables

Phyllo Tarte Tatin

Many of us appreciate the idea of spending hours on a complex and challenging recipe, savouring the results of our efforts and accepting our companions' praises for time and effort well used. Time is so often in short supply, though, and, after all, one need not spend hours in the kitchen to create an enjoyable and special meal. As it happens, there are many uncomplicated main courses on which we can build an impressive dinner in approximately an hour's time.

SIMPLE PLEASURES

Tarte tatin celebrates the cellared autumn apples that sweeten and sustain us.

From years spent working in restaurant kitchens, I have learned that organization is vital to the time-pressed cook. One must plan ahead, shop carefully and maintain an orderly workplace. You can streamline your efforts by keeping a scaled-down version of a professional *mise en place*—the ready-to-go basics that kitchen staff always have at hand—in your kitchen. Finely minced garlic stored in olive oil, chopped shallots, fresh parsley and some freshly squeezed lemon juice all add fast flavour to a meal. I often consider buying pretrimmed meats, and, when my budget allows, I choose tender cuts that are at their best with minimal cooking. Buying vegetables that don't require too much cleaning, trimming and cutting, such as baby carrots, also saves time.

This dinner reflects the unique late-winter spirit of March. Tender lamb satisfies a common seasonal need for comfort, while providing a delicate flavour that heralds the eventual arrival of spring. Fresh rosemary, which is the traditional symbol of remembrance, reminds us of the previous harvest's bounty, and delicate mixed greens anticipate the growing season. *Tarte tatin* celebrates the cellared autumn apples that have sustained us and sweetened our daily lives through the cold. Soon spring will arrive. In the meantime, this meal should help us all to endure the wait.

To save time and stay efficient, I prepare all the dishes at once, pacing myself so that I can easily caramelize the apples while the potatoes boil and bake the tart while I brown the lamb. Use my stopwatch times to gauge your progress.

0:00 Take off your shoes and pour yourself a glass of wine. Then set your timer and start.

0:01 Preheat the oven to 350°F (180°C). Put two medium pots of salted water to boil on the back burners. Wash the potatoes.

For the tart: Place 4 tbsp (75 mL) butter in a stainless steel bowl on the surface of the stove to melt. Peel the apples; core and quarter them if you have a corer, or quarter them and then core them with a paring knife.

0:15 In a 6-inch (15-cm) ovenproof skillet, melt 3 tbsp (45 mL) butter over a high heat; sprinkle sugar evenly over top to caramelize. Cook over a high heat without stirring until the sugar turns light brown. The caramel will be extremely hot, so exercise caution when working with it. Take the pot off the heat and carefully toss the apples in the caramel. Using tongs, arrange the apples in the skillet in concentric circles with rounded sides facing down. Remove the skillet from heat and set it on a trivet next to stove. Cut the phyllo sheets in half horizontally. Pour 3 tbsp (45 mL) melted butter from the stainless steel bowl into a cup to use for brushing pastry. Set aside the remaining butter for vegetables. Layer the phyllo sheets in a crisscross pattern over the apples. Using a pastry brush, paint each sheet with butter before placing the next sheet on top. When all 8 sheets are in place, roll the edges back to form a rim along the inside edge of the skillet. Brush the top and edge with more butter.

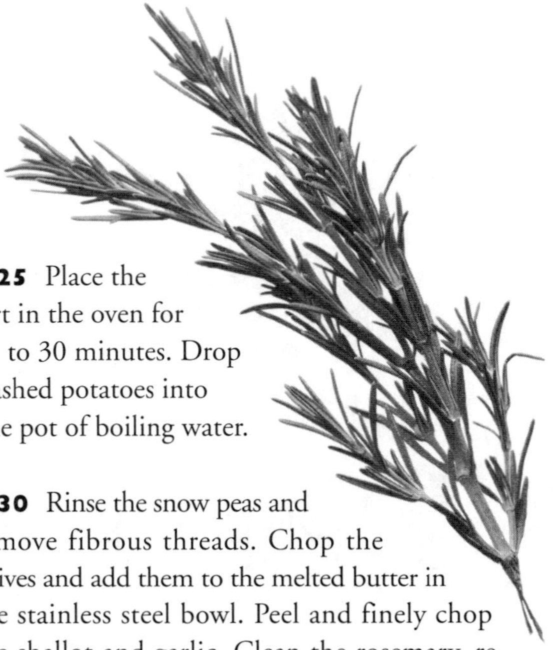

0:25 Place the tart in the oven for 25 to 30 minutes. Drop washed potatoes into one pot of boiling water.

0:30 Rinse the snow peas and remove fibrous threads. Chop the chives and add them to the melted butter in the stainless steel bowl. Peel and finely chop the shallot and garlic. Clean the rosemary, removing leaves from stem. Using a taut length of thread, cut two 1-inch (2.5-cm) thick circles of chèvre and place each one flat side down on a baking sheet. Press 1 tbsp (15 mL) chopped walnuts into each chèvre piece.

For the vinaigrette: In a clean stainless steel bowl, whip 2 tbsp (25 mL) olive oil, vinegar, mustard, and salt and pepper to taste.

0:45 Lightly salt and pepper the lamb. Heat a frying pan over high heat until it is very hot; add 1 tbsp (15 mL) olive oil. Brown the lamb 1 to 2 minutes on each side. Transfer it to a small baking dish. Remove the potatoes from heat but leave them in the hot water to stay warm until they are served.

0:50 Place the lamb in oven. In the frying pan used to brown the lamb, gently sauté the shallot, garlic and rosemary until the shallot softens. Pour in the wine and cook over high heat, stirring to scrape up any brown bits stuck to the pan. Reduce the mixture by half. Turn off the burner and add the whipping cream, salt and pepper to taste. Cover it to keep warm.

0:55 Take the tart out of the oven and set it aside in a warm spot. Place the chèvre in the oven to warm. Toss the mesclun in vinaigrette and divide it between two salad plates.

0:60 Turn off the oven. Remove the chèvre from the oven and place it on top of mesclun. Serve it immediately.

When you are ready to serve the main course, drop the carrots into the other pot of boiling water. After 5 minutes, add the snow peas and boil them for another 1 to 2 minutes. While the vegetables are cooking, slice the lamb thinly on the diagonal, place slices on plates and pour the sauce on top. Drain the vegetables and potatoes and toss them in the melted butter and chives.

If you have leftover Cabernet Sauvignon, serve it with the main course.

To serve the tart, place a warm plate over the top of the frying pan and flip the pan onto plate. Use a rubber spatula to slide out any stray pieces of apple that may have stuck to the pan. Leftover tart can be inverted into the pan and reheated at 325°F (160°C).

Mixed Greens with Chèvre

2 ½ oz (75 g) chèvre
2 tbsp (25 mL) chopped walnuts
2 tbsp (25 mL) olive oil
1 tbsp (15 mL) balsamic vinegar
½ tsp (2 mL) grainy Dijon mustard
Salt and pepper
3 ½ oz (100 g) mesclun (mixed baby salad greens)

Lamb Loins and Sauce

1 shallot
1 clove garlic
1 sprig rosemary
Salt and pepper
2 boneless, pretrimmed lamb loins (thawed overnight, if frozen)
1 tbsp (15 mL) olive oil
½ cup (125 mL) Cabernet Sauvignon
3 tbsp (45 mL) whipping cream

Herbed Vegetables

6 mini new potatoes
1 tbsp (15 mL) butter
10 snow peas
½ lb (250 g) baby carrots, prepeeled
1 tbsp (15 mL) chives

Phyllo Tarte Tatin

6 tbsp (90 mL) butter
3 medium baking apples (such as Granny Smith or Golden Delicious)
¼ cup (50 mL) granulated sugar
4 sheets phyllo pastry, thawed and tightly covered until use

MENU FOR TWO

Mango and Avocado Salad

Coconut Curried Shrimp

Stewed Lentils

Passion Fruit Sorbet
with Rum Sauce

When winter has lost its charm and dreams of a sun-filled vacation have been supplanted by another month of gloom, chase away the blues with exotic foods from southern climes. In this month's 60-minute meal splashes of colour and vibrant tastes brighten your table and your spirits.

TROPICAL DELIGHTS

Chase away the blues with jicama, mango, papaya and passion fruit.

Sometimes the most challenging part of cooking a tropical meal is knowing how to select the produce. Even seasoned travellers can be daunted by the prospect of choosing the perfect mango, and identifying the ideal ripeness of passion fruit can defeat the bravest of shoppers. To guide you, here are tips for buying and storing some of the less familiar fruits and vegetables that are featured in this month's menu.

CHAYOTE Also called christophene, chocho or mirliton, this small, pale yellow-green member of the squash family is best purchased when still firm. Chayote (chy-YO-tay) has a delicate flavour, somewhere between cucumber and zucchini. Peel and core before cooking. Zucchini and summer squash make good substitutes.

JICAMA This Mexican root vegetable (pronounced HEE-ka-ma) is a tan colour and resembles a squat turnip. Choose smaller (more tender) jicama with smooth, thin skin. Peel the skin and the thin fibrous layer underneath. Serve the white, crisp flesh raw in salads or use jicama as a substitute for fresh water chestnuts.

MANGO This oval, round or kidney-shaped fruit originated somewhere near India or Malaysia, but it is now grown throughout the tropics. Use hard green mango for its sour flavour in Asian salads. When serving ripe mango, look for a softer fruit with green, yellow, red or orange tones. Peeling and cutting a mango is a sticky, delicious business: Set the mango on its end and slice through the flesh on either side of the flat, wide pit. Cut each slice into long strips, then cut the skin off each strip. Remove any remaining mango flesh from the pit before discarding it.

Papaya Similar to melon in texture and flavour, papayas are oval or pear-shaped. When ripe, papayas are firm and yield only slightly to the pressure of your hand. Buy golden or green-skinned papayas that feel heavy for their size and have a fresh and fragrant scent. Cut in half lengthwise. Scoop out and discard the black seeds and serve the fruit as an edible dish, allowing diners to spoon out the sweet flesh for themselves. Green, unripe papaya is cooked as a vegetable in Southeast Asia.

Passion Fruit Also called granadilla, the dark purple, red or gold wrinkled skin of passion fruit conceals black, edible seeds and golden pulp. Buy fruit that is heavy for its size, with firm but furrowed skin. Slice off the top and scoop out the seeds and pulp for an instant fruit sauce that's delicious over any dessert.

Star Fruit Also called carambola, this yellow fruit is named for its shape when sliced crosswise. Fortunately, it doesn't need to be peeled; simply wash and slice it for a bright and fanciful garnish (it rarely tastes as good as it looks).

0:00 Open a bottle of Gewürztraminer, a traditional choice for curries.

0:01 *For lentils:* Wash the lentils and pick out any visible debris. Smash 1 clove garlic with the flat side of a large knife; remove the skin. Peel 1-inch (2.5-cm) piece ginger and cut it into pieces large enough to be removed easily later. Combine the lentils, garlic, ginger, water, tomatoes, juice and ½ cup (125 mL) coconut milk in a medium-size pot; bring it to a boil over high heat. Reduce the heat to low and simmer, covered, stirring occasionally, until the lentils have softened, about 40 to 60 minutes. If the liquid cooks off before the lentils are soft, add more water as needed.

0:10 *For the salad:* Cut the papaya in half lengthwise and scoop out and discard the seeds. Cut a thin slice off the bottom of each half so it will sit level; place each one on a plate. Peel the mango and jicama; cut them into long, thin strips. In a small bowl, combine the mango, jicama, coriander and half the lime juice. Lightly season them with sea salt and pepper to taste, then divide the mixture between the two papaya halves. Slice the star fruit, if you're using it, and garnish the plates. Set them aside.

0:20 *To make the rum sauce:* Melt the butter in a saucepan, add the sugar and the mixture cook over medium heat until it begins to bubble. Carefully pour in the rum (it will sizzle) and simmer for 1 minute. Remove the mixture from heat and stir in cream. Set it aside until dessert.

0:30 *For shrimp:* Peel and devein shrimp, leaving the tails intact. Peel ½-inch (1-cm) piece ginger and cut it into thin slices. Peel and roughly chop the shallot and 1 clove garlic. Peel and cut the chayote into thin wedges, discarding the core. Core and slice the red pepper. Heat the oil in a large skillet over medium-high heat; add the ginger, shallot, garlic and curry paste. Sauté for 3 minutes. Add the shrimp, chayote and red pepper. Cook, stirring often, until the shrimp turn pink, 3 to 5 minutes, depending on the size of the shrimp. Pour the wine into the pan and stir, scraping up any bits stuck to the bottom of the pan. Stir in ½ cup (125 mL) coconut milk and simmer 1 minute. Remove the shrimp with a slotted spoon; set aside. Boil the sauce until it is reduced to the desired thickness, 3 to 5 minutes or until it coats the back of a wooden spoon. Add salt and pepper to taste.

Just before serving, peel half the avocado and cut it into thin wedges; arrange them in a fan shape over each stuffed papaya. Reserve the rest of the avocado for another use. Drizzle remaining lime juice over top and season with salt and pepper to taste. Arrange the lentils in a ring on two plates. Place the curried shrimp in the centre, and drizzle with curry sauce and vegetables. Serve with papaya salad.

When you are ready to serve dessert, heat the rum sauce over a medium heat and reduce it to the desired thickness, about 2 minutes. Place a few small scoops of sorbet in two bowls; cover with the sauce. If you're using passion fruit, cut off the top and spoon the seeds and pulp over the sorbet.

Mango and Avocado Salad

1 papaya
1 ripe mango
¼ small jicama
1½ tsp (7 mL) chopped coriander
3 tbsp (45 mL) lime juice
Sea salt and fresh pepper
1 avocado
1 star fruit, optional

Coconut Curried Shrimp

¾ lb (375 g) large raw shrimp
½-inch (1-cm) piece ginger
1 large shallot
1 clove garlic
1 chayote or zucchini
½ red pepper or orange pepper
2 tbsp (25 mL) vegetable oil
1 tsp (5 mL) Thai red curry paste
2 tbsp (25 mL) white wine
½ cup (125 mL) light coconut milk or regular coconut milk
Sea salt and fresh pepper

Stewed Lentils

½ cup (125 mL) red lentils
1 clove garlic
½-inch (1-cm) piece ginger
2 cups (500 mL) water
2 canned plum tomatoes, coarsely chopped
½ cup (125 mL) juice from tomatoes
½ cup (125 mL) light coconut milk or regular coconut milk

Passion Fruit Sorbet with Rum Sauce

1 tbsp (15 mL) butter
1 tbsp (15 mL) brown sugar
2 tbsp (25 mL) rum
¼ cup (50 mL) whipping cream
1 cup (250 mL) passion-fruit sorbet
1 passion fruit, optional

MENU FOR TWO

Caesar Salad

Pesto, Chèvre and
Black Olive Pizza

Tiramisu

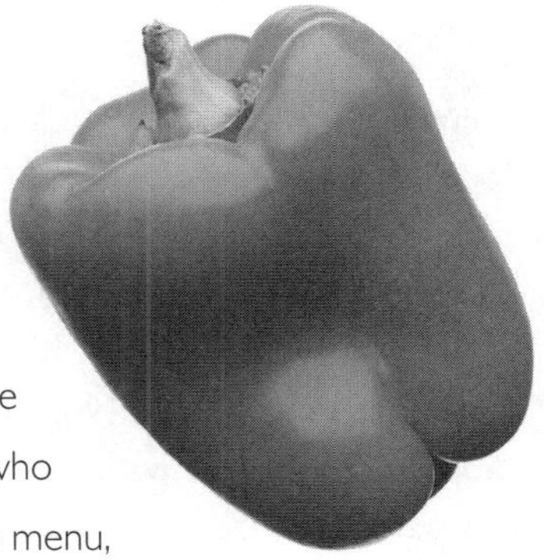

Like most Canadians, I was raised on takeout pizza that tasted more like the cardboard box it arrived in than any type of Italian cuisine. Thankfully times have changed and truly great pizza can be bought or, better yet, made in your own kitchen. Most supermarkets now sell frozen pizza dough, which I prefer over the preformed shells. In our home, we each decorate our own individual pizzas, the tastes of my chef husband and myself varying strongly from those of our toddler, who only eats tomato sauce and cheese. I enjoy something more like the version in this menu, full of savoury flavours and creamy goat's cheese.

A PENCHANT FOR PIZZA

Italian chef Caesar Cardini invented his eponymous salad in the roaring twenties.

When time allows, Bill whips up a batch of his own PIZZA DOUGH using this recipe: Combine ¼ cup (50 mL) warm water with 1 tbsp (15 mL) sugar and 1 tbsp (15 mL) yeast and let stand for 10 minutes. While waiting for the yeast to do its thing, combine 3 cups (750 mL) of flour with 1 tsp (5 mL) salt. Make a well in the flour and add the yeast, 2 tbsp (25 mL) olive oil, 1 tbsp (15 mL) each of finely chopped thyme and rosemary, and 1 cup (250 mL) of water. Mix with a wooden spoon until the dough just comes together. If the dough is too dry, add more water a spoonful at a time. Turn the dough out onto a dusted surface and knead for a few minutes, until it is smooth and pliable. Let it stand, covered with plastic wrap, in a warm spot for 1 ½ hours, then punch it down and roll or toss to desired shape. Prick the bottom of the dough with a fork in several places to keep it from bubbling. This will make two 14-inch (35-cm) pizza crusts and freezes nicely.

Tossing pizza is a skill I don't pretend to possess, but we still make the attempt on pizza nights, just for the fun of it. The idea is to stretch the dough into a circular shape by working it from the centre out using your knuckles, centrifugal force and gravity. I begin by rolling the dough out half way; then I gently spin it, stretching the dough from the centre with my fists. The sides are pulled down by their own weight. As it begins to get larger and rounder, I toss it in the air and as it spins, the dough continues to stretch. It's a good idea to work over a very clean floor, because if you're not an accomplished pizza maker, your dough will likely end up there.

I love a good Caesar salad. It was invented by an Italian, Caesar Cardini, at his Tijuana restaurant in those roaring twenties. Nothing beats a well-made, good, sharp Caesar with plenty of garlic, anchovy and parmesan. Yes, it is a fat black hole, but it's a delicious one. There are concerns, however, about this most venerable of dishes because it is made with raw eggs, which can carry salmonella bacteria.

Handling Eggs

To minimize the risk of salmonella poisoning, always use fresh eggs that have been stored in a refrigerator at temperatures lower than 40°F (4°C). Wash the shell before using the egg to keep any bacteria on the shell from contaminating the egg inside. A fresh egg yolk is round, high and plump; discard any that have deflated and become flat or that have cracked shells. Many cooks coddle the eggs they use for Caesar salad by boiling the whole egg in its shell for 2 minutes and using the slightly warmed, runny yolk. Although coddling helps to thicken the dressing, it could actually increase the bacteria count. Dishes containing raw egg are not recommended by Health Canada and should be avoided by anyone with a weakened immune system, the very young, the elderly and pregnant women. By the way, food manufacturers use pasteurized eggs to make Caesar salad dressing, which reduces the risk of contamination. For more tips about handling eggs safely, go to the Web site of the Canadian Food Inspection Agency at www.cfia-acia.agr.ca or check the phone book for the branch closest you.

Carry me up (which is what *tira mi sù* means in Italian) to a world of divine decadence where rich creamy desserts are served with plenty of nice boozy biscuits and good, strong coffee. Tiramisu is traditionally made with rich mascarpone cheese, which is a triple-cream buttery delight that weighs in at about 45% fat content. My recipe substitutes ricotta at 2% to 5% fat, and the dessert is still delicious. However, if you don't mind the calories and you think tiramisu made without mascarpone is a sin, feel free to slather it on the liqueur-soaked biscuits and enjoy.

0:00 The night before dinner, transfer the pizza dough from the freezer to the refrigerator. Take a Northern Italian (Alto Adige) Chardonnay from your cellar (or nip down to the liquor store) and set it in the refrigerator to chill.

0:01 Take the pizza dough from the refrigerator so it can come up to room temperature.
For the tiramisu: Trim 2 large ladyfinger biscuits to fit the bottom of a mini loaf pan. Soak the cookies with 2 tbsp (25 mL) coffee and 2 tbsp (25 mL) coffee liqueur. The biscuits should absorb all the liquid. Whip the cream until it is stiff. Cream the ricotta and sugar by stirring and pressing them together with a wooden spoon, until the mixture is smooth. Add cinnamon and nutmeg, then stir in whipped cream. Spoon half this mixture over soaked cookies and add a second layer of ladyfingers. Pour the remaining coffee and liqueur over cookies. Spoon the remaining cheese mixture over top and cover with grated chocolate. Place the cake in refrigerator to set.

0:20 *For the pizza:* Gently work the rosemary into the dough. Dust the dough and rolling surface with flour and roll it out to fit a 12-inch (30-cm) pizza pan. (See previous page for instructions on tossing pizza dough.) Squish the plum tomatoes and mix in pesto. Brush a pizza pan with oil, place the dough on the pan and perforate it with a fork; brush the dough with oil. Spoon the tomato mixture evenly over the dough. Cut the red pepper into thin strips and arrange them over sauce. Dab chèvre evenly around the pizza. Pit the olives and scatter them over the pizza. Preheat oven to 450°F (230°C).

0:50 *To prepare the salad:* In a large salad bowl, mince the garlic and mix it with anchovy paste. Whip in the egg yolk. Add the lemon juice and whip until light and fluffy. Slowly whip in the olive oil. This is the tricky part—if you add the oil too quickly, the dressing will break. Stir in the parmesan, and salt and pepper to taste. Cut or tear lettuce into bite-size pieces and toss them in dressing until they are nicely coated. Stir in the croutons. Place the pizza in the middle rack of the oven to bake for 10 to 12 minutes or until the bottom of the crust is golden brown. Serve the salad and pizza along with some smooth Tony Bennett.

Caesar Salad

1 clove garlic
1 dab anchovy paste or 1 anchovy, finely chopped
1 egg yolk
½ tsp (2 mL) lemon juice
¼ cup (50 mL) olive oil
2 tbsp (25 mL) grated parmesan
Sea salt and fresh pepper
1 romaine heart
⅓ cup (75 mL) croutons

Pesto, Chèvre and Black Olive Pizza

10 oz (300 g) pre-made frozen pizza dough
2 tbsp (25 mL) chopped fresh rosemary
2 tbsp (25 mL) flour
½ cup (125 mL) canned plum tomatoes
¼ cup (50 mL) pesto
2 tbsp (25 mL) olive oil for brushing
½ red pepper
3 oz (90 g) chèvre
14 black olives

Tiramisu

4 large ladyfinger cookies
¼ cup (50 mL) strong coffee or espresso
2 tbsp plus 2 tsp (35 mL) Kahlua or coffee liqueur
⅓ cup (75 mL) whipping cream
⅔ cup (150 mL) ricotta cheese
1 tbsp (15 mL) sugar
Pinch cinnamon
Pinch nutmeg
2 tbsp (25 mL) grated chocolate

MENU FOR TWO

Pissaladière

Roasted Rack of Lamb

Wine Braised Red Cabbage
with Raisins

Chocolate Mousse

No room for idle chitchat today. I have so many tips and recipes to pass on that I'm going to get right to the meat of the matter. Premade tapenade is now widely available, but if there is time try making your own using the recipe below, which makes a sharp tapenade with plenty of garlic and lemon.

LAMBTASTIC!

> *This chocolate mousse is sinfully rich and delightfully easy to make.*

For a tasty TAPENADE, start with good olives. Removing the pits is tedious work but can be done in half the time by squeezing them out rather than trying to cut them out. Combine in a food processor ½ cup (125 mL) pitted black olives, 2 cloves garlic, 2 anchovies, 1 tbsp (15 mL) capers, 2 tbsp (25 mL) fresh parsley, 1 tbsp (15 mL) lemon juice and 2 tbsp (25 mL) olive oil. Blend until a smooth paste forms. Makes a little more than ½ cup (125 mL).

Puff pastry is another item that can, mercifully, be purchased easily, and it makes a lovely pissaladière. However, once again, if time permits I prefer to use this buttery short pastry. One of the best things about making my own pastry is that it allows for personal touches. I add thyme and dried chilies; similar amounts of any herbs or flavouring, such as finely diced sundried tomatoes, will work equally well. A benefit of using puff pastry is that leftover dough can be rerolled and made into fanciful cinnamon twists to use as garnish for the chocolate mousse.

To make your own SHORT PASTRY, combine 1 cup (250 mL) flour, a pinch salt, 1 tbsp (15 mL) fresh chopped thyme and 1 tsp (5 mL) dried chilies. Rub in ¼ cup (50 mL) cold butter, cut into small cubes, until the texture is like tiny pebbles. Add 1 egg, beaten, and 2 tsp (10 mL) cold milk, and then mix until the dough just comes together. Let rest, covered, for 20 minutes. Roll out to just under ¼-inch

(6-mm) thickness, then cut and garnish as directed for the puff. Bake at 425°F (220°C) for 12 to 15 minutes or until edges and bottom are golden. This recipe makes four pissaladière shells. The dough can stand being rerolled once and freezes nicely.

For CINNAMON TWISTS, roll out the leftover puff pastry. Cut dough into ½-inch (1-cm) strips and brush them with melted butter. Sprinkle sugar and cinnamon liberally; twist each one and then bake them at 400°F (200°C) for 5 to 7 minutes or until they are golden.

The chocolate mousse presented here is sinfully rich and delightfully easy to make. Whipped egg whites, which are usually added to a mousse, are omitted here, saving time in the preparation and setting stages. Melting the small amount of butter and chocolate on the stovetop saves the step of setting up a bain marie. A bain marie is traditionally used to melt the chocolate slowly over an even heat: too high or uneven heat can result in a dull, grainy product, but I find a warm stovetop works just as well for small quantities of chocolate.

0:00 Take the pastry from the freezer to thaw 1 hour before beginning. Preheat oven to 400°F (200°C) 15 minutes prior to start. Open a bottle of Cabernet Sauvignon, for the sauce and the saucier.

0:01 *For the mousse:* Whip the cream in a narrow container and store it in refrigerator. Place the butter and chocolate chips in a stainless steel bowl on the stove surface to melt. (If your oven has a stay-cool surface, melt the chocolate over hot, not boiling, water.) In a small pan over high heat, reduce the sugar in ¼ cup (50 mL) water until it has a syrupy consistency that coats the back of a spoon, about 3 minutes. In another narrow container (a tall yogurt container works well), whip the egg yolks with the hot syrup until it is very light and fluffy, about 5 minutes. If the chocolate mixture is not fully melted, stir it with a rubber spatula until it is smooth. Whip the egg into the chocolate. Fold in the whipped cream until the consistency is even; spoon into two large wine glasses and chill.

0:20 *To prepare pissaladière:* Roll out the pastry so it is 1/16 inch (1.5 mm) thick. Cut out two 5- to 6-inch (12.5- to 15-cm) circles and place them on a non-stick baking tray. Spread 2 tsp (10 mL) tapenade evenly onto each circle. Make very thin onion rings by slicing four full rounds from the red onion. Separate the rings and place them on tapenade. Cut two thin slices of tomato and place them over the onions. Cut each anchovy into three thin strips and fan over the tomato slices. Set pissaladières aside. Place them on the middle rack of the oven to bake for 15 minutes before you're ready to serve them.

0:35 *For the lamb:* Mix together the rosemary, salt and peppercorns. Remove the fat cap from the lamb, leaving a thin layer for crisping, and cut away any obvious silver skin. Look for a hard, white or yellowish line of fat at the bottom edge of the meat; if it is present, cut it away. Press the herb mix into the lamb and cut the meat into two portions. (If there are only seven bones, make one portion the three bones at the thicker end of the rack and the other portion the four bones at the thinner end.) Cover the bones with foil to prevent them from burning and put the meat fat side up in an open baking dish with short sides; place the dish in the top third of the oven. For medium–well-done lamb, bake for 20 minutes, then broil for the last 3 to 5 minutes if the fat requires extra crisping. You want a thin layer of browned, crisp fat just covering the meat. When the meat is done, brush off any rosemary that burned in the broiling and cover with a tent of aluminum foil; let the meat rest for 5 minutes, then cut into the rack vertically between the bones, three quarters of the way through. This leaves the rack attached but makes it easier for diners to handle on the plate.

0:50 *To prepare cabbage:* Thinly slice 8 oz (250 g) of cabbage from the head. Place duck fat in a medium-size frying pan or sautoir over high heat until it begins to smoke. Add the cabbage and cook, stirring, until it softens, about 5 minutes. Add the wine and raisins and reduce the heat to simmer. Let the mixture simmer for 10 minutes while you enjoy the pissaladière. Season to taste, and then use tongs to transfer the cabbage from the pan to the plate, leaving excess liquid and some of the raisins behind. Pour the liquid and remaining raisins into the lamb pan and deglaze over medium heat by using a wooden spoon to scrape up any hard bits from the bottom. Quickly stir in 1 tsp (5 mL) of cold butter and when the mixture is reduced to a sauce-like consistency, pour it over the lamb and serve.

Pissaladière

4 oz (120 g) puff pastry
4 tsp (20 mL) tapenade
4 slices red onion
2 slices tomato
2 anchovies

Roasted Rack of Lamb

1 tbsp (15 mL) chopped fresh rosemary
1 tsp (5 mL) coarse sea salt
1 tsp (5 mL) crushed mixed peppercorns
1 rack of lamb (8 bones, cleaned and frenched, with chine bone off)

Wine-Braised Cabbage

1 head red cabbage
3 tbsp (45 mL) olive oil or duck fat
¾ cup (75 mL) Cabernet Sauvignon
2 tbsp (25 mL) raisins
Pinch cayenne
Sea salt and fresh pepper
1 tsp (5 mL) cold butter

Chocolate Mousse

¾ cup (75 mL) whipping cream
2 tsp (10 mL) butter
¼ cup (50 mL) semi sweet chocolate chips
1 tbsp (15 mL) sugar
2 egg yolks

MENU FOR TWO

Poached Artichokes with
Garlic Mayonnaise

Magret of Duck with Rhubarb
and Cherry Chutney

Herb-Roasted Sweet Potato
and Parsnips

Chocolate Bourbon
Pots-de-Crème

The warm winds of April signal spring's arrival, when temperate weather and longer days mix memory and desire, "stirring dull roots with spring rain" (apologies to T. S. Eliot). In keeping with the season, this month's menu features foods with flavours to stir your winter-weary senses.

SPRING INDULGENCES

The artichoke's rep as an aphrodisiac once rendered it improper food for ladies.

Dinner begins with one of springtime's earliest vegetables, the artichoke. Its reputation as aphrodisiac once rendered it unthinkable as proper food for ladies, which did not stop Catherine de Medici from indulging. Legend has it she nearly died from a surfeit of artichokes, consumed, appropriately enough, on her wedding day.

The artichoke's thorny exterior may seem the antithesis of sensual allure, but the art of eating this thistle is not: When each leaf has passed between the teeth, its tender heart is exposed and the soft, supple inner leaves must yield to the bite. (Repressed Victorian women, one assumes, could not be trusted to keep their bustles in order once exposed to such powerful charms.)

To follow the artichoke, we propose tender, pink breast of duck (a fillet cut known in French as a *magret*) served with a chutney of early rhubarb and dried cherries. For a perfect *magret*, I like to melt away all the fat over moderate heat, so that the flesh lies right against a thin, crisp layer of succulent skin. Treated with care, this is one of the nicest and quickest ways to prepare duck.

The dessert in this menu combines two of the world's best-loved indulgences: chocolate and bourbon.

Wine connoisseur Sebastian Van Merendonk suggests a dry Riesling or a Sauvignon Blanc, if white suits your fancy. Among reds, look for a Beaujolais Grand Cru such as a Moulin à Vent or an Oregon Gamay.

A meal is more than the sum of its ingredient list. Remember the story of *Like Water for Chocolate:* It's the cook's emotion, first and foremost, that makes food irresistible.

0:00 Put on something inspiring—music that is. Dance a little.

0:01 Preheat the oven to 425°F (220°C). Wash the sweet potato and peel the parsnips. Cut each in half lengthwise, then cut the halves into ½-inch (1-cm) thick wedges. In a mixing bowl, toss the sweet potato and parsnips lightly in olive oil and dried fines herbes; scatter the wedges in a roasting pan and place them in the oven. Stir occasionally.
For the artichokes: In a medium saucepan on the back burner, combine 8 cups (2 L) water, ⅓ cup (75 mL) lemon juice and salt; place over medium-high heat and cover. Bring to a boil.

0:10 *For the custard:* In a saucepan over medium-high heat, combine the cream, milk and vanilla. In a heatproof bowl, whisk together the sugar with the yolks and whole egg. When the cream mixture is hot, add the bourbon and then stir in the chocolate chips. When the chocolate is melted, gradually whisk the cream mixture into the egg mixture. Pour into two 3 ½-inch (175-mL) ceramic custard cups. Reduce oven temperature to 300°F (150°C).

0:20 Place the filled custard cups in a deep baking dish in the oven and pour enough hot water into the dish to come halfway up sides of the cups (this technique is often referred to as bain-marie cooking, and its purpose is to prevent delicate dishes from becoming tough or dry during baking). Set the timer for 35 minutes. In a saucepan, bring the apple juice and raspberry vinegar to a boil. Reduce heat. Using a sharp knife, chop the top quarter off each artichoke. Break or cut off the stems. Immerse artichokes in boiling water and weight with a small lid or heatproof plate. Reduce heat to a simmer.

0:30 Chop the rhubarb and mince 1 clove garlic. Add both to the hot vinegar mixture, along with dried cherries, citron, cayenne, nutmeg and allspice. Let the mixture simmer over low heat. To prepare the garlic mayonnaise, in a food processor purée 2 cloves garlic with the mayonnaise, remaining lemon juice and a pinch cayenne.

0:45 Put a heavy frying pan over high heat. Score each duck breast and place them skin side down in hot pan; immediately reduce heat to medium. Remember, you want to cook off the fat and crisp the skin without burning it. Drain fat every 5 minutes. If you have a fat screen, place it over the pan.

0:50 Check the rhubarb mixture. Remove it from the heat when the liquid is reduced by at least half and is the consistency of a chutney.

0:55 When the timer goes off, remove custard cups from oven and place them on counter to cool. Turn off the oven. Check the duck. When the skin is crisp and the fat has cooked away, turn the breasts over and sear the other side for 1 to 2 minutes. Turn off the heat, cover and let rest. The duck will still be pink. Remove the artichokes from poaching water and turn off the burner. (An artichoke is done when you can pull a leaf easily from the stem.) For well-done duck, place meat in a baking dish and leave it in the warm oven until you are ready to serve it.

0:60 Serve the artichoke whole with the garlic mayonnaise on the side, or see the sidebar for how to remove the choke before serving. Next, serve the duck, sliced on the diagonal, with a stripe of chutney and frisée, if you're using it, and the roasted sweet potato and parsnips straight from the oven. For dessert, place the custard cups on plates and surround each cup with fresh raspberries.

Disarming the Artichoke

- Add lemon juice to poaching water—its acidity stops artichokes from browning.
- Mature artichokes are thorny, so chop off their tops with a knife or trim their thorns with scissors before working with them.
- Artichokes have a hairy, inedible choke at their centre. You can either serve the artichoke whole (give your guests a spoon so that they can remove the choke themselves) with a dipping sauce on the side, or you can remove the choke after cooking and use the artichoke to hold the accompanying sauce.
- To remove the choke, insert a pair of tongs (or your fingers) in the centre of a trimmed, cooked artichoke. Remove inner leaves and reserve. Then use the square end of the tongs or a spoon to scrape away the hairy choke, taking care not to damage the heart beneath. Discard the choke.
- To serve, invert reserved leaves and return them to the artichoke centre. Fill it with mayonnaise, vinaigrette, or melted butter and lemon juice.
- To eat, remove the leaves one at a time, dip them into the accompanying sauce and use your teeth to scrape off fleshy part. Discard the rest of the leaf.

Poached Artichokes with Garlic Mayonnaise

⅓ cup (75 mL) plus 1 tsp (5 mL) lemon juice
1 tsp (5 mL) salt
2 medium artichokes
2 cloves garlic
½ cup (125 mL) mayonnaise
Pinch cayenne

Magret of Duck with Rhubarb and Cherry Chutney

1 cup (250 mL) apple juice
⅓ cup (75 mL) raspberry vinegar
1 cup (250 mL) fresh rhubarb
1 clove garlic
½ cup (125 mL) dried cherries
2 tsp (10 mL) candied citron
Pinch each cayenne, nutmeg and allspice
1 to 2 boneless duck breasts with skin
Handful frisée, optional

Herb-Roasted Sweet Potato and Parsnips

1 large sweet potato
3 medium parsnips
1 tbsp (15 mL) olive oil
2 tsp (10 mL) dried fines herbes

Chocolate Bourbon Pots-de-Crème

½ cup (125 mL) whipping cream
½ cup (125 mL) homogenized milk
½ tsp (2 mL) vanilla
¼ cup (50 mL) granulated sugar
2 egg yolks
1 whole egg
4 tsp (20 mL) bourbon
½ cup (125 mL) chocolate chips
½ cup (125 mL) fresh raspberries

MENU FOR TWO

Beet Carpaccio

Spinach Gnocchi with Gorgonzola Sauce

Raspberry White-Chocolate Puffs

There are many steps to take on the road to becoming a chef. First comes the realization that food is much more than sustenance; for me, it has long been a fascination, perhaps even an obsession. While others may be intrigued by world events, fashion or the arts, I am consumed by culinary curiosities. Visiting an art gallery, I question the ripeness of Cézanne's apples. When confronted with da Vinci's *The Last Supper,* I look to see what the disciples are eating. For me, the secret of the Caramilk bar is not just a silly advertisement. I need to know—how does one coat caramel with chocolate?

THE SAUCIER'S APPRENTICE

My dinner with André featured his most popular dish: gnocchi.

After a couple of years spent working as a kitchen slave in the mid 1980s, I discovered that impossibly long hours, hard physical work and holidays spent with a stockpot rather than family were somehow acceptable to me. So I enrolled in culinary school. Next, I looked for a chef with whom I could study, which brings me to my dinner with André. In my case, this does not refer to the film classic, but to the countless nights I spent as an apprentice in the kitchen of André Théberge at André's Restaurant in Toronto. The kitchen was small and most days it was just the two of us, preparing for dinner in the afternoon, then cooking for the evening rush.

The gnocchi featured in this month's menu was André's most popular dish (and his legacy to me), so here it is, for your enjoyment. I have made some alterations; as André was naturally thin, and French too, his food tended to be impossibly high in fat. While customers could eat this dish again and again in blissful ignorance, it is a harder thing to knowingly cook such a rich dish for yourself.

Just in case you, like André Théberge, think low-fat cuisine is absurd, here is the original GORGONZOLA SAUCE from André's Restaurant. In a small saucepan over low heat, reduce 1 cup (250 mL) whipping cream until it is thick like a sauce, and stir in 2 tbsp (25 mL) gorgonzola cheese. Season with a pinch each of salt, cayenne, freshly grated nutmeg and freshly ground pepper.

My wine choice for this meal is an old Amarone, but if this is hard to find or prohibitively expensive, try a young Barbera, a red wine with enough acidity to marry well with the lemon in the beets, or a full-bodied Pinot Grigio—the round tones and fruity crispness of this white wine pairs well with cream sauces.

0:00 Let your taste buds or your concerns about your waistline decide between the original full-fat version of the gorgonzola sauce and the more conservative rendition.

0:01 Preheat oven to 375°F (190°C). To make the puffs, roll out the pastry to an 8- x 5-inch (20- x 12-cm) rectangle; cut this into two 4- x 5-inch (10- x 12-cm) pieces. Cut a smaller rectangle out of the centre of each piece to create two 1-inch (2.5-cm) rectangular frames. Place the frames and centre pieces on an ungreased baking sheet, spaced well apart. Bake 7 to 10 minutes until they are golden. Remove the sheet from oven and set it aside to cool.

0:05 *For the gnocchi:* In a large saucepan over a high heat, bring 2 ½ cups (625 mL) salted water to a boil. Wash the spinach and remove any large, tough stems. Place the spinach in the boiling water and cover. Blanch 2 to 3 minutes or until the leaves are wilted. Drain and rinse the spinach under cold water. Press it to remove most of the water, and then wrap it in cheesecloth or a clean kitchen towel and squeeze until the spinach is very dry. This is crucial; if the spinach is too moist, the gnocchi will fall apart, so squeeze it until you think you cannot possibly get out any more water, and then squeeze a little more. Finely chop the spinach. In a medium bowl, mix the spinach with ricotta, 2 tbsp (25 mL) flour, 1 egg yolk and a pinch each sea salt, cayenne, nutmeg and pepper. Sprinkle the remaining flour on a baking sheet. Dust your hands with flour and form 1-inch (2.5-cm) balls out of the spinach dough. Coat the balls with flour, place them on a tray and refrigerate them.

0:35 To assemble the dessert, place the white chocolate in a stainless steel bowl over hot, not boiling, water until it melts. Whisk in the sour cream. Place each pastry frame on a dessert plate. Fill the centre with a pyramid of raspberries. Lean the centre squares along one side and drizzle the white chocolate sauce over the berries and pastry. Refrigerate until you are ready to serve it.

0:45 *For the carpaccio:* In a medium bowl, whisk together the lemon juice, olive oil, sugar, and sea salt and pepper to taste. Peel the beet; cut it crosswise into paper-thin slices (use a mandolin if you have one). Toss the beet slices in the dressing and arrange them on two plates in concentric circles. Set aside.

0:50 *For the gorgonzola sauce:* In a small saucepan over high heat, stir together 1 tbsp (15 mL) flour and 1 tbsp (15 mL) butter until the paste (the roux) begins to brown. Whisk in ¼ cup (50 mL) milk; continue whisking until the mixture is smooth and free of lumps. Whisk in the remaining milk. When it begins to bubble, slowly add wine, stirring, and then reduce the heat to simmer. Let the sauce thicken to the desired consistency. Stir in the gorgonzola and a pinch each salt, cayenne, nutmeg and pepper. Keep the sauce warm until ready to serve.

Just before serving the beets, peel and core the apple. Grate it or slice it into matchsticks. Pile the apple in the centre of each plate of beet rounds. Garnish with parmesan shavings and coarsely ground pepper to taste. Serve immediately.

For the gnocchi: In a large saucepan, combine 6 cups (1.5 L) salted water and ½ cup (125 mL) white vinegar and bring to a boil. Once the liquid boils, reduce the heat to simmer. About 10 minutes before you're ready to serve the main course, poach the gnocchi in the simmering water for 10 minutes or until they are hot through to the centre. (If necessary, raise heat to maintain a simmer.) Remove them with a large slotted spoon and let excess water drain off onto a clean tea towel. Divide the gnocchi between two plates and top with the sauce.

Beet Carpaccio

3 tbsp (45 mL) lemon juice
1 tbsp (15 mL) olive oil
¼ tsp (1 mL) granulated sugar
Sea salt and fresh pepper
1 medium beet
1 medium apple
1 tbsp (15 mL) parmesan shavings

Spinach Gnocchi

2 ½ cups (625 mL) salted water
10 oz (300 g) fresh spinach (1 to 2 bunches)
¾ cup (175 mL) ricotta
½ cup (125 mL) flour
1 egg yolk
Pinch each sea salt, cayenne, freshly grated nutmeg, fresh pepper
6 cups (1.5 L) salted water
½ cup (125 mL) vinegar

Gorgonzola Sauce

1 tbsp (15 mL) flour
1 tbsp (15 mL) butter
¾ cup (175 mL) milk
¼ cup (50 mL) white wine
2 tbsp (25 mL) gorgonzola
Pinch each sea salt, cayenne, freshly grated nutmeg, fresh pepper

Raspberry White Chocolate Puffs

¼ block (50 g) frozen puff pastry, thawed at room temperature for 1 hour
2 oz (60 g) white chocolate, chopped
3 tbsp (45 mL) fat-free sour cream, at room temperature
½ pint (250 mL) fresh raspberries

MENU FOR TWO

Capellini with Fresh Herbs
and Parmesan

Roasted Chicken Frittata

Walnut Oat Cakes

I have always been attracted to people who cook. When I was six, my very first boyfriend and I spent considerable time making mud pies together. The thing I remember most about him was that he bought me my first gift from an admirer—a Creamsicle. My first serious relationship as a teenager was with a young man who worked weekends at the local steak house. I will never forget the thrill I felt whenever Chef would allow me into the kitchen. Chef was an impressive man, French, physically imposing and possessing a talent for knife work. As I stood in the corner of the bustling kitchen, making myself as small as could be, I was dazzled by his hands as he deftly boned fish, chopped mushrooms at breakneck speed and brought his massive cleaver down to sever bones like a hammerhead. I wanted to have that kind of power.

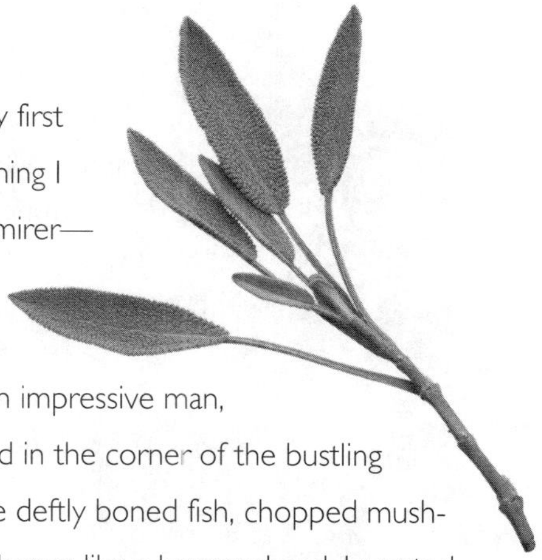

MEN IN WHITES

Brighter days and lighter moods call for a fresh, clean wine. Open a bottle of Pinot Blanc.

A dozen years later, in culinary school, I met my husband, Bill. It was not his baby blue eyes, his muscular upper body or his sweet little derrière that turned my head. No, it was his ability to turn out strudel pastry, the way his forearm angled just so as he whisked his perfect hollandaise. And, of course, his knife work was stunning. So, we have lived happily ever after, cooking, eating and exploring the vast culinary world together. Arguments in our house are more likely to be patched up over a stock pot than a dozen flowers, and a romantic evening always features food as a main attraction.

There is no end to the benefit I derive from having a chef husband. One small example is the Walnut Oat Cake featured in this menu. I tasted a wonderful cake while I was touring farms in Ontario's Mennonite country and, of course, I bought a second piece to bring home to Bill. Actually, I ate the second piece and so bought a third. I made the first attempt at duplicating the recipe, which turned out too eggy and wet. I spent the rest of the afternoon in my office, dimly aware of

Bill moving about the kitchen. Toward the end of the day, he appeared, baby blue eyes and all, in the doorway with a plate of steaming hot cake. Even better than the one I had tasted on the farm.

This menu is a perfect example of the simple yet tasty kind of food we like to prepare at home. After a long day spent cooking in a professional kitchen, we look for menus that don't require too much fuss or time spent at the stove. However, we would rather go hungry for an evening than have to ingest something lacking in flavour. So an uncomplicated pasta followed by a light frittata suits us just fine. The dessert requires little effort and offers a hearty and satisfying close to the meal. In fact, I find these cakes so satiating that I have been known to skip the rest of the meal and enjoy this dessert alone, with no accompaniment other than a cup of hot tea.

0:00 Brighter days and lighter moods call for a fresh, clean wine. Open a bottle of Pinot Blanc (or Catherine's choice of a young Italian Trebbiano or Pinot Grigio) and try to recapture the mood of mudpie making.

0:01 *For cakes:* Preheat oven to 350°F (180°C). Whip together eggs and sugars until they are frothy. Add milk and molasses. Stir in oats and walnuts. Pour into two buttered 1 ½-cup (375-mL) ceramic baking dishes. Bake on the middle rack of the oven for 20 minutes or until the cakes spring back to the touch. When you're ready for dessert, drizzle maple syrup over top the cake and serve.

0:15 *For pasta:* Bring 6 cups of salted water to boil. Chop the herbs and dice the shallots (do all the shallots at once). Reserve half the shallots for the frittata. Mince the garlic.

0:25 *For the frittata:* Chop the chicken and red pepper into ½-inch (1 cm) pieces. Slice the mushrooms. This is a great opportunity to use up leftover bits of chicken, by the way. In a nonstick oven-safe 10-inch (25-cm) pan, sauté the peppers, mushrooms and shallots in oil until they are soft. Set the pan aside. In a bowl, whisk the eggs with water and mustard and sprinkle with sea salt and fresh pepper. Place the bowl in the refrigerator until you are ready to cook the frittata.

0:40 *For the pasta:* Heat the oil over medium-high heat and add butter. Sauté the shallots, herbs and garlic until just toasted. Drop the pasta in boiling water and stir it gently to break up the nests. Let it cook for 2 to 3 minutes or until the pasta is tender but firm to the bite. Drain, sprinkle with salt and toss in herbs and butter, fluffing the pasta gently with a fork. Serve it immediately with plenty of fresh parmesan and pepper.

After enjoying the pasta, finish the frittata: Place the pan with vegetables over a medium heat and add the chicken.

When the mixture is hot, pour in the eggs and cook, stirring, until the eggs begin to come together. Dab the cheese over top and place the pan in the oven. Let it cook until the eggs are cooked and fluffy and the cheese is melted, about 5 to 7 minutes. Serve immediately.

Capellini with Fresh Herbs and Parmesan

¼ cup (50 mL) fresh herbs (choose anything you like —I use basil, oregano and sage)

¼ cup (50 mL) shallots

1 clove garlic

2 tbsp (25 mL) olive oil

2 tbsp (25 mL) butter

Sea salt

4 oz (120 g) dry capellini nests

¼ cup (50 mL) grated parmesan

Fresh pepper

Roasted Chicken Frittata

¼ cup (50 mL) shallots

3 oz (90 g) roasted chicken

¼ red pepper

4 oz (120 g) crimini mushrooms

1 tbsp (15 mL) olive oil

4 eggs

2 tbsp (25 mL) water

½ tsp (2 mL) Dijon mustard

Sea salt and fresh pepper

2 tbsp (25 mL) chèvre

Walnut Oat Cakes

2 eggs

2 tbsp (25 mL) brown sugar

2 tbsp (25 mL) white sugar

¼ cup (50 mL) milk

1 tbsp (15 mL) molasses

¾ cup (75 mL) quick cooking oats

¼ cup (50 mL) walnuts

2 tbsp (25 mL) maple syrup

MENU FOR TWO

Pappa al Pomodora

Zucchini Parmigiana

Creamy Polenta

Warm Arborio Rice Pudding

Pappa al Pomodora, or Bread Soup, was first introduced to me by my husband by way of his experience in the kitchen at Coco Lezzone in Toronto's Little Italy. I immediately added this hearty and simple dish to my file of foods to make when the cupboard is bare. Stale bread, some onions, garlic and tomato become a hearty solution to the question of what to cook when there is nothing to cook. This soup is traditionally made with beef or chicken stock, which provides a deep, richness of flavour. It is possible to adapt the ingredients to accommodate a vegetarian diet, but the vegetable stock needs to be fortified with a little miso. This Japanese bean paste is a mainstay of my meatless repertoire. The darker-coloured paste is extremely full flavoured, lending round tones and deep flavour to dishes that might otherwise be a tad insipid. High in protein and B vitamins, it also packs a nutritional punch. A final note about this soup: better quality bread makes a better, more flavourful soup.

POMODORA, PARMIGIANA, POLENTA AND PUDDING

As in life, timing is everything here: polenta must be cooked just prior to serving.

To make a quick and easy VEGETABLE STOCK, cover 1 lb (500 g) bean sprouts with cold water, bring to a boil, then simmer for 15 minutes and strain. Stir in 1 to 2 tbsp (15 to 25 mL) miso.

When I was composing this menu, I actually had a yen for Eggplant Parmigiana. But, just as Rome was not built in a day, neither can Eggplant Parmigiana be built in under an hour. So for those weekends when there is a little more time to play in the kitchen, try my recipe for Eggplant Parmigiana. When time is precious, the zucchini parmesan offered here is a great substitute for fast and furious cooking, taking all of 10 minutes to assemble.

To make EGGPLANT PARMIGIANA, cut one large eggplant into ¼-inch (6-mm) slices. Sprinkle 1 tbsp (15 mL) salt over top, weigh the slices down with a dish or a book, and let them drain for 2 hours. Wash the slices in cold water and dry them with paper towels, pressing out as much moisture as possible. In one bowl, beat 2 eggs, and in another bowl, place 1 cup (250 mL) bread crumbs; dredge each eggplant slice first in the egg and then in the bread crumbs. Fry the slices in hot olive oil until they are golden brown on both sides. Layer fried eggplant in a 2-quart (2-L) casserole dish with 2 cups (500 mL) tomato sauce, ½ lb (250 mL) sliced mozzarella and 1 cup (250 mL) grated parmesan, finishing with the cheeses. Bake, uncovered, for 30 minutes or until the cheese is brown on top. This dish serves four.

In these columns, as in life, timing is everything. The polenta, for example, must be cooked just prior to serving, so it requires that the cook spend 10 or 12 minutes stirring in between courses. If relaxing with the meal is a greater priority, you can serve the zucchini and polenta first and follow them with the soup course.

0:00 This meal requires a good deal of stirring, so warm up your arm by patting yourself on the back for taking this hour out of your hectic schedule to enjoy cooking. Preheat oven to 400°F (200°C).

0:01 *To make the pudding:* Bring 2 cups (500 mL) salted water to boil. Add the rice and boil for 5 minutes. Meanwhile, in a medium saucepan, heat 1 cup (250 mL) milk, sugar, raisins, cinnamon, nutmeg, vanilla, butter and nut liqueur until the mixture begins to bubble. Drain the rice and stir it into the milk. Reduce the heat to simmer and cook, stirring, until the milk is absorbed into the rice. Add another ⅓ cup (75 mL) milk and stir until it is absorbed. Add the remaining milk and remove the saucepan from the heat. Set it aside until you are ready to serve dessert.

CATHERINE'S WINE TIP

Absolutely a Cabernet Franc! Or a blend of Cabernet Franc and Merlot from the New World. This is a good opportunity to shop locally—for example, some Ontario vineyards are producing a stellar wine with these grapes.

0:20 *To start the soup:* Thinly slice the onion and smash the garlic, removing the skin. In a medium saucepan, sauté them in oil over medium high heat, until they are brown. Roughly chop tomatoes. Cut bread into ten 2-inch (5-cm) squares. Add the bread, stock and tomatoes to pan and bring to a boil. Reduce heat to simmer, cover and let cook for 20 minutes. This produces a very thick, hearty soup; however, if the bread absorbs all the stock, add an additional ¼ to ½ cup (50 to 125 mL) stock and bring it to a boil just before pouring into soup bowls. Garnish with chopped sage and parmesan.

0:35 *For Zucchini Parmigiana:* Butter a medium loaf pan and trim the bread so it lines the bottom. Whip the egg with the cream and sprinkle with sea salt and fresh pepper. Cover the bread with the egg mixture and let it soak in. Cut the zucchini into thin, wide slices. Place the following layers on the bread: one third of the mozzarella, 2 tbsp (25 mL) parmesan, zucchini to cover. Sprinkle with more salt and pepper and repeat so there are three layers in total, finishing with zucchini. Mix the tomatoes, wine and pesto together and pour over top. Cover with bread crumbs and the remaining cheese. Bake, uncovered, for 25 to 30 minutes or until the egg has set and the top is brown and bubbly.

0:50 *To begin the polenta:* Chop the onion. Cook it in butter, in a small pan, until soft. Add the stock and bring it to a boil. Remove the pan from the heat. *Between courses:* Return the stock to boil. Stir in the cornmeal quickly to prevent it from sticking. Reduce the heat. Be careful as the polenta will splatter if the heat is too high. Continue stirring for 10 minutes, until the polenta is creamy and thick. Garnish with parmesan and serve immediately.

To finish dessert: Place the pan back on high heat, stirring, until the rice is hot. Serve in two dessert bowls, garnished with cinnamon sticks and powdered sugar.

Pappa al Pomodora

½ small onion
3 garlic cloves
1 tbsp (15 mL) olive oil
1 cup (250 mL) canned plum tomatoes
2 2-inch (5-cm) slices very stale, hard bread
2 ¼ cups (550 mL) chicken or vegetable stock
2 tbsp (25 mL) fresh sage
2 tsp (10 mL) grated parmesan

Zucchini Parmigiana

2 slices bread
1 egg
2 tbsp (25 mL) whipping cream
Sea salt and fresh pepper
1 zucchini
4 oz (120 g) sliced mozzarella
⅓ cup (75 mL) grated parmesan
¼ cup (50 mL) canned plum tomatoes, drained
¼ cup (50 mL) red wine
1 tbsp (15 mL) pesto
1 tbsp (15 mL) bread crumbs

Creamy Polenta

¼ small onion
1 tbsp (15 mL) butter
1 ¼ cup (300 mL) vegetable or chicken stock
¼ cup (50 mL) cornmeal
1 tbsp (15 mL) grated parmesan

Warm Arborio Rice Pudding

⅓ cup (75 mL) arborio rice
1 ⅔ (400 mL) cups milk
2 tbsp (25 mL) sugar
2 tbsp (25 mL) raisins
¼ tsp (1 mL) cinnamon
Pinch nutmeg
½ tsp (2 mL) pure vanilla extract
1 tbsp (15 mL) butter
1 tbsp (15 mL) nut liqueur
2 cinnamon sticks
1 tsp (5 mL) powdered sugar

MENU FOR TWO

Fiddleheads and Asparagus
in Sorrel Sauce

Lobster with Orange
Tarragon Butter

Citrus-Scented Rice

Tomatoes Provençales

Strawberries and Chantilly Cream

This quick-to-prepare main course celebrates the flavours of a dish so popular that both sides of the Atlantic want to take credit for it. One legend has it that lobster *à l'américaine* was invented by a 19th-century expatriate French chef who whipped up the dish for some late-night American customers. If you believe *Larousse Gastronomique*, the recipe instead has its origins in Brittany, or Armorica, and its true name is lobster *à l'armoricaine.*

TRANSATLANTIC TREAT

"It's like drinking stars."
– Monk Dom Perignon, after first tasting Champagne.

I have simplified the preparation of this popular dish to accommodate quick cooking at home, but elements of the traditional, more elaborate version remain: Tarragon, butter, tomato, garlic, shallots and citrus each make an appearance.

Anyone who knows classical French cooking might protest that I have omitted the brandy from my adaptation of the lobster dish. This is to achieve a lighter, simpler effect ideal for spring.

To precede this rich main course, I have concocted a tart dish of fiddleheads and asparagus dressed in sorrel sauce. Fresh fiddleheads, the unfurled tops of young ferns, are only available in springtime. Should you wish to collect your own, make sure you know which ones to look for; all fiddleheads are not equal in taste. If you are cooking them out of season, look for the frozen version.

Sorrel is a delicate leafy green, resembling spinach in appearance, with a distinctly lemony flavour. It is primarily used as seasoning in cooking. If you have any leftovers, small ribbons of sorrel make an excellent addition to any salad. Don't make a steady diet of the raw leaves, though; like raw spinach, they are mildly toxic when eaten in excessive quantities.

The dessert, a layering of bright red strawberries, store-bought pound cake and vanilla-laced cream, makes a simple end to a full-flavoured meal.

"It's like drinking stars" is the reputed utterance of everyone's favourite monk, Dom Perignon, when he first tasted Champagne. I suggest Veuve Clicquot for its full-bodied characteristics. If champagne is not to your liking, try a Muscadet de Sèvre et Maine sur lie. This wine is allowed to rest on its lees (a sediment of dead yeast cells and grape particles) before bottling, which imparts extra flavour, freshness and a light carbonation.

It has recently become fashionable to drink red wine with seafood, but it is important to choose carefully. Avoid heavy wines that are high in tannins. Instead, try a lighter-bodied burgundy such as a Santenay or Mercurey and you will be rewarded with a happy marriage of tastes.

Lobster and champagne. Strawberries and cream. Why not? You deserve it.

0:00 Relax. Breathe and meditate on the joys of time spent in your kitchen.

0:01 Preheat the oven to 350°F (180°C). Finely dice 2 shallots and 2 cloves garlic. Set half of them aside for the tomatoes.
For the rice: In a small- to medium-size saucepan with a tight-fitting lid, heat 1 tbsp (15 mL) olive oil over a high heat. Lightly brown the remaining shallots and garlic in oil. Add basmati rice and stir until it is coated with olive oil and lightly warmed. Add 1 cup (125 mL) water and ¼ tsp (1 mL) salt. Add the orange halves and the orange and lemon zest. Cover. Listen for a full rolling boil. Turn off the burner. The rice will steam itself over the hour.

0:10 *For the dessert:* Cut each slice of pound cake into one 3-inch (8 cm) square and one 2-inch (5 cm) square. Sprinkle each with 1 tbsp (15 mL) liqueur and set them aside.

For the tomatoes: Mix the reserved shallots and garlic with 1 tsp (5 mL) olive oil, bread crumbs, 2 tbsp (25 mL) grated parmesan and parsley. Slice the tomatoes in half horizontally. Salt and pepper to taste. Press the mixture into the tops of tomato halves. Place them cut side up in baking dish, and set aside.

0:25 Put water on to steam the fiddleheads and asparagus.
To make the sorrel sauce: In a food processor, purée, until emulsified, ⅓ cup (75 mL) olive oil, mustard, sorrel and 2 tbsp (25 mL) grated parmesan. Slowly add 2 tbsp (25 mL) lemon juice; mix well. Salt and pepper to taste.

0:30 To butterfly the lobster tails, use kitchen shears. Working toward the fan-shaped bottom end, cut a straight line through the middle of the shell and meat, about two thirds deep. Leave the tail end attached and pull the meat up through the cut in shell so that it sits on top. Rub the meat with 1 clove garlic. Segment the orange. Place 1 sprig tarragon, 1 tbsp (15 mL) butter and 1 segment of orange into the slit in each lobster tail. Reserve the remaining orange segments for the butter. Place the lobster tails on a baking sheet and set aside.

0:40 Put the tomatoes in oven for 30 minutes. Using a mixer, whip cream and vanilla until fluffy. *Voilà!* Chantilly cream.

0:45 Hull the strawberries and slice each in half. Spread a quarter of the chantilly cream onto the two large squares of pound cake. Arrange half the strawberries, rounded side up, on top of the cream. Spread more cream on one side of the 2-inch (5 cm) squares and centre, cream side down, on top of the berries. Add nearly all the remaining cream and top with berries. Refrigerate the desserts and leftover cream.

0:50 Rinse the fiddleheads and asparagus. Break off the woody ends of asparagus. Place the fiddleheads and asparagus in steamer. Melt ½ cup (125 mL) butter over low heat. Coarsely chop 2 sprigs tarragon and reserved orange segments, and stir them into the butter. Salt and pepper to taste. Gently whip the sauce and it keep warm.

0:57 Remove the fiddleheads and asparagus from the steamer and serve with the sorrel sauce.

0:60 Place the lobster in the oven and roast 10 minutes. When the meat is no longer translucent, dress it with orange tarragon butter and serve it with rice and tomatoes. Before serving dessert, top each dish with the remaining cream.

Fiddleheads and Asparagus in Sorrel Sauce

⅓ cup (75 mL) olive oil
¼ tsp (1 mL) Dijon mustard
4 leaves sorrel
2 tbsp (25 mL) grated parmesan
2 tbsp (25 mL) lemon juice
Sea salt and fresh pepper
1 cup (250 mL) fiddleheads
8 spears asparagus

Lobster with Orange Tarragon Butter

2 lobster tails, thawed
1 clove garlic
1 orange, peeled
4 sprigs tarragon
½ cup (125 mL) plus 2 tbsp (25 mL) butter
Sea salt and fresh pepper

Citrus-Scented Rice

1 shallot
1 clove garlic
1 tbsp (15 mL) olive oil
½ cup (125 mL) basmati rice, washed repeatedly
¼ tsp (1 mL) salt
1 orange, halved
Zest of ¼ each orange and lemon

Tomatoes Provençales

1 shallot
1 clove garlic
1 tsp (5 mL) olive oil
2 tbsp (25 mL) bread crumbs
2 tbsp (25 mL) grated parmesan
1 tbsp (15 mL) fresh parsley, chopped
2 tomatoes
Sea salt and fresh pepper

Strawberries and Chantilly Cream

2 (½-inch/1-cm) slices pound cake, cut lengthwise
4 tbsp (50 mL) hazelnut liqueur or another flavoured liqueur
¾ cup (175 mL) whipping cream
¼ tsp (1 mL) vanilla extract
10 to 12 strawberries

MENU FOR TWO

Warm Scallop Salad

Nori-Wrapped Chicken

Tossed Soba Noodles

Spa Greens

Mixed Berries with
Vanilla Yogurt

In my world, whipping cream makes a good sauce better, cooking in butter is preferable to anything and chocolate exists for a reason. However, warmer weather makes the idea of lighter foods more palatable, and even I contemplate cooking foods that are lower in fat, calories and sodium at this time of year. But can food be both lean and luxurious? Both slimming and succulent?

LOW-FAT FABULOUS FUSION

Wasabi, nori and pickled ginger adds an Asian punch to chicken.

Flavour is the key. We all love fat, sugar and salt because they brighten flavours and enhance taste. When cooking *sans gras,* the trick is to use other, less sinful flavour builders. Herbs, spices, infused vinegars, fresh juices and the vibrant tastes of ginger, garlic and onion are all excellent fat-free choices. Rich, homemade stock also goes a long way toward making a light sauce with minimal fat. The homemade variety can be reduced to a dark, thicker broth with a more intense flavour. Store-bought bouillon can replace it in a pinch, but bouillon tends to be high in sodium and monosodium glutamate. In any form, chicken stock is lighter in flavour and more versatile than other meat stocks and is my favourite for all-round use.

In low-fat cooking, familiarity sometimes breeds contempt. Light versions of your favourite recipes, such as mock chocolate mousse or macaroni and danbo cheese, often fall short of expectations. So instead of recasting old standbys, I turn to international ingredients to add an eclectic twist to the meal. For this menu, I borrowed from Japanese cuisine, which traditionally uses much less animal fat than European cooking. I have added a little punch to a simple chicken dish with wasabi (Japanese horseradish), nori (seaweed wrappers used for sushi) and pickled ginger.

The healthiest drink to accompany the meal is water with a twist of lemon. Refreshing, crisp, unassuming and always a good vintage, it is the drink of choice for the slimming set.

0:00 *For the dessert:* Wash the berries and set aside. Place the yogurt in a small serving bowl. If the yogurt is very thick, stir in some apple juice. Refrigerate.

0:05 *To prepare the chicken:* Place the chicken pieces on a plate. In a cup, mix together 1 tbsp (15 mL) soy sauce and wasabi; pour the mixture over the chicken. Place a layer of 1 tbsp (15 mL) pickled ginger on top each chicken piece. Dip each sheet of nori in a shallow pan of warm water to soften it, and then wrap a sheet around each chicken piece. Place the wrapped chicken on a nonstick baking sheet and refrigerate.

0:10 *For the noodles:* In a medium saucepan, add 1 cup (250 mL) homemade stock and bring it to a boil over high heat; simmer, uncovered, until reduced by half. (Alternatively, bring ½ cup/125 mL canned stock to a simmer over medium heat; do not reduce.) In another saucepan, bring 6 cups (1.5 L) water to a boil. Meanwhile, cut the garlic into thin slices and chop green onions. Add the garlic and green onions to the chicken stock; let simmer. Drop the noodles into boiling water and cook, stirring occasionally, for 6 to 8 minutes or until just *al dente.* Drain the noodles and rinse them under cold water. Add the noodles and 1 tsp (5 mL) soy sauce to simmering stock. Remove saucepan from heat; set aside.

0:30 *To make the greens:* Quarter the endive lengthwise. In a skillet with a tight-fitting lid, bring 1 cup (250 mL) stock to boil; add lemon juice. Reduce the heat to simmer and add the endive. Let the mixture cook, covered, 10 minutes; remove it from heat. Preheat oven to 375°F (190°C).

0:40 *For the scallop salad:* Wash and dry the mesclun. Arrange the salad on two appetizer plates. Rinse the scallops and pat them dry with paper towel. In a dry nonstick pan cook them over medium heat for 2 to 3 minutes on each side. (If using smaller bay scallops, cook for 1½ minutes each side.) Scallops should be opaque and lightly browned on the outside and hot in the centre. Arrange cooked scallops on greens. Return the pan to medium-high heat and deglaze it by adding wine, vinegar and tarragon. Let sauce reduce by a quarter. Whisk in the olive oil and pour the sauce over salads. Add salt, if desired.

Scallops are delicious when slightly raw in the middle, but for safety reasons health officials suggest cooking them through.

0:50 Place the chicken in the oven for 15 minutes. Meanwhile, serve the scallop salad. When you are ready to serve the main course, quickly reheat the noodles and endive in their pans over high heat. Drain them. Divide noodles between two plates and arrange the endive quarters around them. Slice each chicken roll in half on the diagonal, if desired, before arranging it on noodles.

When you are ready for dessert, assemble the fruit salad: Place mixed berries in waffle cups, if you're using them, or in two bowls. Peel the kiwifruit, cut it lengthwise into wedges and place them around the circumference of the bowl. Top each dish with yogurt and garnish with mint sprigs and a tuile, if you're using them.

Warm Scallop Salad

3 cups (750 mL) mesclun (baby greens)
5 oz (140 g) large sea scallops or bay scallops
¼ cup (50 mL) white Zinfandel wine
1 tbsp (15 mL) raspberry vinegar
1 tbsp (15 mL) chopped tarragon
1 tsp (5 mL) olive oil
Sea salt, optional

Nori-Wrapped Chicken

2 pieces (4 oz/120 g each) boneless, skinless chicken breast
1 tbsp (15 mL) light soy sauce
1 tsp (5 mL) wasabi paste
2 tbsp (25 mL) pickled ginger
2 sheets seasoned nori

Tossed Soba Noodles

1 cup (250 mL) homemade chicken stock or 1/2 cup (125 mL) canned chicken stock
6 cups (1.5 L) water
2 cloves garlic
2 green onions
3 oz (90 g) soba noodles (Japanese buckwheat noodles)
1 tsp (5 mL) light soy sauce

Spa Greens

1 large Belgian endive
1 cup (250 mL) homemade chicken stock or diluted canned chicken stock
2 tbsp (25 mL) lemon juice

Mixed Berries with Vanilla Yogurt

1 cup (250 mL) mixed berries
5 tbsp (75 mL) low-fat vanilla yogurt
2 tbsp (25 mL) apple juice, optional
2 waffle cups or 2 tuiles (curled wafer cookies)
2 kiwifruit
2 to 4 sprigs mint

MENU FOR TWO

Three Pea Salad

Sole-Wrapped Sea Scallops
with Blackcurrant Reduction

Broccolini Parcels

Banana Split

I maintain that most diets fail due to a lack of banana splits. It is simply not reasonable to expect a person to survive *sans* chocolate. I have no intention of even trying. However, the slight but steady weight gain that often accompanies the more sedentary winter months does give one pause. Summer will be here soon enough and with it comes the desire to wear as few clothes as possible. So, if I want to fit into any of last year's capri pants, a reducing diet is the bitter pill I must swallow. Again, bitter pills always go down easier with a little chocolate. Therefore, in an attempt to make spring slimming work, I have devised my spa spectacular split *d'ananas* using a small serving of low-fat ice cream graced with plenty of fresh fruit and a sprinkling of chocolate chips. It is amazing how a few little chips make all the difference between feelings of sunken-cheeked deprivation and jolly memories of happy childhood seconds stolen at the soda fountain.

THE BANANA SPLIT DIET

A "spa split" consists of low-fat ice cream, fresh fruit and a sprinkling of chocolate.

I am currently writing the Canadian version of Brigit Légère Binns' *The Complete Idiot's Guide® to Low-fat Cooking,* which has an entire chapter dedicated to fish: Fishing for Compliments. Why so much fish? Because it is a nutritional boon to dieters and a fantastic source of lean protein. I lost 50 pounds about 12 years ago by eating a diet heavy in fish, fresh vegetables and fruit. Fish also has a prominent place in *Nice Timing* because its delicate flesh cooks quickly and adapts well to uncomplicated recipes. Salmon, scallops, mussels, mackerel, shrimp and lobster have all been featured in the magazine column, prepared in fast, flavourful ways.

There are three primary elements to plate design: height, unity and colour. Food presented without consideration to these factors can look bland and unappealing or chaotic and even frightening. Too much is as detrimental to the final design as is too little, and when cooking spa cuisine, presentation becomes even more important. Again, the secret to success is to avoid feeling deprived. So if portions are a little small, make up for it by preparing yourself something lovely. This menu—with its pristine white fish set off nicely on a background of black current reduction, accompanied by crisp green and red broccolini parcels, and finished with some fanciful red confetti—is aesthetically pleasing and will assuage any feelings of being underfed.

Pamper the eye and pamper the stomach.

0:00 The unique tastes of the world's only banana split diet await you. Preheat the oven to 375°F (190°C).

0:01 *To make the salad:* Clean the snow peas by the removing tips and the fibrous thread that runs along the side of the pod. Wash the peas and pea sprouts. Pat them dry with a paper towel and place them in a salad bowl. *To make the dressing:* Whisk together the vinegar and salt until the salt is fully dissolved. Whisk in the oil until the mixture is fully emulsified. When you are ready to serve the salad, toss the greens in the dressing and serve them on two appetizer plates. The sole and the broccolini will not sit well after cooking, so I suggest serving them as the first course and following with the salad course.

0:15 *To prepare the fish:* Gently wash the sole fillets and pat them dry. Sprinkle them with sea salt and fresh pepper. Place two scallops in the centre of the skin side of one of the filets. Roll the fillet around the scallops and secure with a long toothpick; repeat with the remaining scallops and fillet. Pour the wine and lemon juice into a 5-inch (12.5-cm) square pan or a medium loaf pan. Place the fillets in the baking dish and set on the medium rack of the oven for 15 to 20 minutes or until the scallops are firm, white and hot throughout. Cut the unpeeled ginger into thin slices and place them in a small saucepan with the blackcurrant juice. Bring the mixture to a boil; then lower the heat to simmer and let the liquid reduce until it coats the back of a spoon. Remove the ginger.

CATHERINE'S WINE TIP

Here, I think a New World white, a Fume Blanc, will link the tastes of the meal yet allow them to remain distinctive.

0:35 *For the broccolini:* Put 6 cups (1.5 L) salted water on to boil for broccolini. Trim the ends of broccolini stems. Shave most of the flesh from the inside of the red pepper and cut two 1½-inch (3.5-cm) strips from the skin. Chop the remaining red pepper into very small (1/16-inch/1.5-mm) diced confetti. When the water boils, drop the red pepper in and cook it until it is soft and pliable, about 1 minute. Remove the red pepper using tongs and refresh it in cold water—this will set the colour. Place the broccolini in the boiling water and blanch for 3 to 5 minutes or until it is tender but crisp. Drain and make two bundles of four spears each; then wrap a red pepper strip around each bundle. A dab of butter will enhance the taste of the vegetable, but if you are being very, very good, a little squeeze of fresh lemon will do. When all is hot and ready, divide the blackcurrant reduction between two plates and carefully transfer the sole from the

dish to the plates. Use a lifter to move the sole as it will want to come apart. Place a broccolini parcel at the side of each roll and decorate it with red pepper confetti. Cut the lemon into four thick wedges and place two on each plate.

After dinner, assemble the banana split: A banana split boat goes a long way to recapturing some of the childhood thrill of indulging in this fun dessert. Quarter the banana lengthwise so there are four long wedges. Fit two wedges into either side of each boat. Make four small ice-cream balls and place them in centre of the boat. Cover with washed berries, chocolate chips and marshmallows. Long soda spoons help to make the image complete.

Three Pea Salad

1 handful snow peas
½ cup (125 mL) green peas, fresh or thawed
1 handful pea sprouts
1 tbsp (15 mL) tarragon vinegar
¼ tsp (1 mL) sea salt
1 tbsp (15 mL) extra virgin olive oil

Sole-Wrapped Sea Scallops with Blackcurrant Reduction

2 sole fillets, approximately 3 oz (90 g) each
Sea salt and fresh pepper
4 sea scallops
2 tbsp (25 mL) white wine
2 tsp (10 mL) lemon juice
1 piece (2 inch/5 cm) ginger, peeled
⅔ cup (150 mL) unsweetened blackcurrant juice
1 lemon

Broccolini Parcels

8 spears broccolini
¼ red pepper
Lemon or butter

Banana Split

1 banana
½ cup (125 mL) fat-free ice cream, any flavour
½ cup (125 mL) fresh mixed berries
1 tbsp (15 mL) chocolate chips
1 tbsp (15 mL) mini marshmallows

MENU FOR TWO

Cucumber Buttermilk Soup

Chicken Breast Poached
in Tomato and Pepper Ragout
with Zucchini and Eggplant

Angel Food Cake
with Lemon Sauce

Buttermilk, in great-grandma's day, was a byproduct of butter churning. When nothing was wasted in the kitchen, this was the liquid that remained after the churning, and it was prized for making pancakes, scones, muffins and a dish out of the southern American States called chess pie. An ideal dairy product for fat-conscious dieters, 1 cup (250 mL) of buttermilk contains only a trace of fat and little more than 50 calories. The appetizer course in this menu pairs the tangy goodness of buttermilk with the fresh flavours of cucumber and mint for a delicious, fat-free, chilled soup.

HEAVENLY ANGEL FOOD

Let them eat cake.
I cannot emphasize
enough the importance
of dessert to a good diet.

When cooking *à la spa,* I tend to prepare dishes like the chicken featured here because, as all the ingredients slowly cook together, their flavours are intensified and this richness of flavour is what is often lacking in low-cal cuisine. This recipe also gives me the opportunity to use eggplant—a terrific vegetable high in calcium and low in calories that I often pass by because I haven't the time to prepare it. Usually, eggplant is salted and pressed for an hour before cooking to reduce its bitterness, but here it is sautéed and then slowly baked.

One of my favourite methods for cooking EGGPLANT comes from an old Russian family recipe of my friends the Wolfsons. First, poke a few holes into four eggplants, then bake them at 400°F (200°C) for 45 minutes or until they are soft. Remove the pulp and chop it, along with 2 onions and 2 carrots. Sauté the mixture in ½ cup (125 mL) olive oil until the eggplant is brown, and then add 2 cups (500 mL) chopped tomatoes and ¼ cup (50 mL) tomato paste. Cook the whole thing down until it turns into a paste, about 10 to 20 minutes, stirring constantly. Stir in 2 tsp (10 mL) salt, ½ tsp (2 mL) paprika, ¼ tsp (1 mL) chili peppers and 5 minced cloves of garlic. Cook this lot for an additional minute or two, and then stir in ¼ cup (50 mL) sour cream. I love serving this as a dip or spread—any that survives the meal gets refrigerated to use in sandwiches the next day. A word to the wise: this is not a low-fat dish!

Let them eat cake. Once again, I cannot emphasize enough the importance of dessert to a good diet—in this case, a light, guilt-free, fat-free angel food cake. Aptly named, this sponge cake was obviously brought to earth by a heavenly messenger posing as a baker in order to lessen the load of dieters the world over. Yes, there is still plenty of sugar in the cake but perhaps if you don't tell your fat cells they won't notice. You could choose to eat a moderate portion, fully aware that you are consuming some sugar but still happy to nosh on a little cake that has been made without butter, egg yolks or fat-happy chocolate. The amazing angel food cake is leavened purely by the chemical reactions of air and steam, and it is a little more temperamental than most of the other desserts featured in *Nice Timing.* If this is your first attempt at this celestial treat, take heart; the recipe presented is as simple as it sounds. You do, however, need to be a little fussy: the eggs must be cold; the containers, utensils and pans must be squeaky clean; the whites must be mixed on medium and just until the soft peak stage, when they are getting firm but the peaks are rounded; you must be very gentle when folding the flour into the whites; and the cake must be inverted immediately upon removal from the oven. These are the cake angel's five commandments and if followed they will result in absolute success.

CATHERINE'S WINE TIP

How about an inexpensive Shiraz? I like the weight and character to go well with this meal, but don't spend too much money; a young wine will do. In fact the tomatoes in the menu will kill a more expensive, delicate vintage.

0:00 First churn some butter, then use the remaining liquid to make soup. Or pour yourself a glass of Shiraz because at my spa, we drink wine and eat cake. Preheat oven to 375°F (190°C).

0:01 *To prepare the chicken:* Heat the olive oil over medium high heat, in a medium oven-safe pot or a 2-quart (2-L) stovetop-safe casserole dish. Chop the onion and cook it in oil until it is soft. Cut the peppers, zucchini and eggplant into 1-inch (2.5-cm) cubes and chop the garlic; add the vegetables and garlic to the onions and sauté until they are slightly browned. There is very little oil in the pot, so the vegetables will stick a little—if they stick too much or the bottom gets too brown, move on to the next step: Deglaze the pan with red wine by scraping any bits from the bottom of the pan with a wooden spoon. Then add the drained tomatoes and salt. Bring the mixture to a boil and then add the chicken. Spoon the vegetables over the chicken and place the dish in the oven to bake for 50 to 60 minutes or until the chicken is very tender and the vegetables and liquid have reduced.

0:20 *For soup:* Roughly chop the cucumber and green onion. Combine all the soup ingredients in the bowl of a food processor and pulse until they are fully blended. Place the bowl in refrigerator to chill, along with two soup bowls. When you are ready to serve the soup, ladle it into the chilled bowls and place a mint-leaf garnish in the centre of each.

0:40 Stir the chicken and vegetables to make sure the chicken stays moist.

For the cake: Reduce oven heat to 350°F (180°C).

To make lemon sauce: Stir the milk into the icing sugar slowly until it forms a thin paste. Stir in the lemon extract. There should be just enough sauce to drizzle over the top of the finished cakes. Set it aside. Sift together the flour, salt and nutmeg. Rinse the bowl and utensils that you will use for the egg whites first in vinegar and then in cold water and dry them with a clean towel. On the medium setting of your mixer, whip the cold egg whites with lemon and vanilla extracts until the mixture reaches the ribbon stage. Add the sugar and continue to whip until soft peaks form. Do not over-whip. Sift the flour into the whites, folding in with very gentle motions, in four batches. Gently spoon the batter into two ungreased mini angel food cake pans and set them on the middle rack of the oven. Bake for 7 to 10 minutes or until lightly browned on top and an inserted toothpick comes out clean. Immediately invert the cake pans so the cakes can cool upside down. This helps the cakes defy gravity—otherwise they may fall. Let the cakes cool until dessert, and then gently them urge away from the sides of the pan and tap the bottom until they come out. Serve each whole small cake with lemon sauce drizzled over top.

Cucumber Buttermilk Soup

1 cup (250 mL) buttermilk
½ English cucumber
1 green onion
2 sprigs fresh mint (about 20 small leaves)
2 stems fresh thyme
½ tsp (2 mL) salt
1 tsp (5 mL) lemon juice

Chicken Breast Poached in Tomato and Pepper Ragout with Zucchini and Eggplant

1½ tsp (7 mL) olive oil
½ cooking onion
½ green pepper
½ red pepper
1 zucchini
½ eggplant
1 clove garlic
¼ cup (50 mL) red wine
1 28-oz (796-mL) can plum tomatoes, drained
½ tsp (2 mL) sea salt
2 10-oz (280 g) chicken breasts, skinless, bone in

Angel Food Cake

½ cup (125 mL) sifted cake flour
Pinch salt
Pinch nutmeg
3 egg whites, cold
Pinch cream of tartar
½ tsp (2 mL) vanilla
½ tsp (2 mL) lemon extract
¼ cup granulated sugar

Lemon Sauce

2 tbsp (25 mL) icing sugar
1 tsp (5 mL) milk
2 drops lemon extract

SUMMER

Take one large grassy field, one half dozen children, three small dogs, and walk along a narrow strip of brook, pebbly if possible. Mix the children with dogs, and empty them into the field, stirring constantly. Sprinkle the entire area with daisies and buttercups, pour brook gently over pebbles, and cover all with a deep blue sky and bake in hot sun for several hours. When children are thoroughly browned, they may be removed.

–*Mrs. Estes,* Buck's County Cookbook

Sweet summer provides the opportunity for abandoning the kitchen for the barbecue. A capon breast is skewered on a piece of sugarcane, a New York strip loin sizzles to perfection, and grilled shrimp is served with an insouciant salsa. Greek *mezedes* are ideal for turning a simple meal into a feast for friends. The sweet courses in these menus range from the effervescence of cherries jubilee to the simple succulence of grilled pineapple.

Fresh homegrown foods require little in the way of adornment or manipulation: very little cooking with heat goes on in the following pages. Dandelion greens are served in a cold pasta salad alongside a many-layered muffuletta, and the convenience of a store-bought roasted chicken makes assembling a picnic that much easier. These menus are designed to get you out of the kitchen and into the great backyard, or anywhere the birds are singing and the air is fresh.

MENU FOR TWO

Tuscan White Beans
on Arugula

Orzo with Truffle Oil

Portobello Mushroom Tower

Cheese Course

For most Canadians, truffles are a mysterious and decidedly foreign thing. They call to mind trained pigs rooting through the dank, ancient forests of Périgord, France, or Italy's Umbria. At $1.50 per gram for the Italian black variety, this is not a food we are prepared to eat every other Tuesday. Still, once tasted, the distinctive and singular aroma and flavour of truffles haunt you until you can no longer deny the craving despite the cost.

MAD FOR MUSHROOMS

> *Simple dishes can be elevated to the spectacular with a few drops of truffle oil.*

The good news is that this fungus is more accessible than ever. Fresh truffles, truffle oil and truffle butter are now available across Canada. A favourite is white truffle oil, which often comes in an 8 fl oz (240 mL) bottle (about $40), but also can be found in smaller quantities. Minuscule amounts of the oil add a distinctive taste to pastas, meats, salads and eggs. Eggs benedict can be elevated to the spectacular with a couple drops of truffle oil in the hollandaise. In this month's meal, a spoonful of truffle oil imparts its heady flavour to an orzo pasta dish with crimini and porcini mushrooms.

Beyond Umbria's truffle forests, our first course relies on the neighbouring hills of Tuscany for inspiration. Extra virgin olive oil is a hallmark of Tuscan cuisine. In a marinade, dressing or sauce, its characteristic flavour is often present and always welcome. Also central to this region's cooking is the humble and wonderful white bean, which in this recipe must soak overnight before it is paired with arugula.

TRUFFLES

The official truffle season lasts from December 1 to March 1. Truffle oils and butters can be enjoyed year-round. Professional chefs often dilute truffle oil with extra virgin olive oil (in a ratio of 1 to 3) to make this oil with its heady aroma more affordable. Bury fresh truffles in rice and store them in a sealed container, but eat them within days of purchase. If you use arborio rice you can make a stunning truffled risotto afterward. Or keep unbroken eggs in a sealed container with a truffle overnight; when you cook the eggs, you will be pleasantly surprised by the taste. The village of Sainte-Alvère in France has an excellent Web site (www.sainte-alvere.com) where you can learn more about this musky delicacy.

We need not stray outside Tuscany for this month's wine selection. Chianti has just the balance of vivacity and warmth required for truffles and nothing goes better with portobello mushrooms. Look for a Chianti Classico Riserva, which is aged for three years (generally in oak casks), giving it a complex and robust character.

When you serve a cheese course, try to select a variety of mild to strong flavours and soft to hard textures. Keeping this in mind, feel free to substitute these choices with any of your favourites. As it ages, robiola lombardia changes from soft and sweet to a semihard cheese that has a distinct truffle-like flavour. If you have difficulty finding it, substitute taleggio. German cambozola imitates Lombardy's famous gorgonzola, but its flavour is softened with the milder qualities of camembert. For a stronger, more traditional choice, serve gorgonzola. Either will complement asiago, a hard cheese with a sharp flavour.

0:00 My favourite music for preparing *la cucina italiana* is Gary DeMichele's score from the movie *Big Night,* but any of your favourite arias should get you in the mood.

0:01 Take the cheeses out of the fridge to warm. Drain the beans and place them in a pot with 4 cups (1 L) water. Bring to a boil, then simmer uncovered 45 minutes. (Don't salt the beans until after they soften.) Wash arugula, portobellos, tomato, grapes and pears, and dry them on paper towels. Remove portobello stems and reserve them for another use. Wipe the crimini and porcini with a damp paper towel.

0:15 Cut 2 rounds each from the widest part of the tomato and onion. Each slice should be ⅓ inch (8 mm) thick and similar in circumference to portobello tops. Remove the robiola rind. Place cheese atop the tomato; set aside.

0:25 Preheat oven to 350°F (180°C). Slice crimini and porcini mushrooms, but leave the portobello tops whole. Chop the red pepper into ½-inch (1-cm) dice.

For bean dressing: In a stainless steel or glass bowl (the acid in lemon juice picks up flavour from plastic or pottery), whisk together 2 tsp (10 mL) garlic, 3 tbsp (45 mL) lemon juice and ½ tsp (2 mL) salt. When the salt has dissolved, add ⅓ cup (75 mL) extra virgin olive oil. Arrange the arugula on two appetizer plates and set aside. Arrange the cheeses and grapes on a wooden cheese board and set aside. Place biscotti on a separate plate.

0:40 Brush the portobello mushrooms and onion with olive oil, lightly salt them and place them on a deep baking sheet in the oven. Boil 8 cups (2 L) water with 2 tsp (10 mL) salt for the orzo.

0:45 Drain the beans and toss them with the dressing. Place them on arugula and garnish with red pepper.

For the orzo: Sauté 2 tsp (10 mL) garlic and sliced mushrooms in 2 tbsp (25 mL) olive oil. Cover to keep warm.

0:50 Turn portobellos and onions. Serve Tuscan beans.

0:60 Between courses, put the tomato and cheese on a baking sheet and place it in the oven; turn off the heat. The residual heat will keep the vegetables hot and melt the cheese. Boil the pasta for about 8 minutes; stir occasionally. Strain it and toss it with sliced mushrooms. Drizzle with truffle oil. Salt and pepper to taste. In the centre of each plate, layer towers thus: portobello, red onion, portobello, tomato and cheese, and portobello. Skewer each tower with a sprig of rosemary. Surround with orzo and serve. Before the cheese course, slice the pears.

Tuscan White Beans on Arugula

½ cup (125 mL) dried cannellini beans, soaked overnight in water
1 bunch arugula
½ red pepper, seeded
2 tsp (10 mL) minced garlic
3 tbsp (45 mL) lemon juice
½ tsp (2 mL) salt
⅓ cup (75 mL) extra virgin olive oil

Orzo with Truffle Oil

2 cups (500 mL) fresh porcini and crimini (brown) mushrooms
2 tsp (10 mL) salt
1 cup (250 mL) orzo pasta
2 tsp (10 mL) minced garlic
2 tbsp (25 mL) olive oil
1 tbsp (15 mL) truffle oil

Portobello Mushroom Tower

6 medium portobello mushrooms
1 large tomato
1 large red onion
2 large slices Robiola or Taleggio
1 tbsp (15 mL) olive oil
Sea salt
2 3- to 4-inch (8- to 10-cm) sprigs rosemary

Cheese Course

3 oz (90 g) asiago
3 oz (90 g) cambozola or gorgonzola
3 oz (90 g) aged Robiola or Taleggio
1 small bunch green grapes
1 small bunch red grapes
2 Bartlett pears
4 almond biscotti

MENU FOR FOUR

Grilled Meze Platter with Accompaniments

New Potato Salad with Wild Greens

Honey-Dipped Fruit and Nuts

From the cradle of civilization to the comfort of your own backyard, this month's menu celebrates prime grilling season with the pure and simple flavours of Greece. Olive oil, plenty of fresh lemon, herbs and garlic (the "stinking rose") lend robust character to grilled calamari, fennel, green tomatoes, artichokes and a salad of wild greens. Hot and cold, sweet and savoury, this meze ("appetizer") platter features tasty nibbles to be enjoyed in the garden or on the balcony, while sipping Retsina and sharing laughter and good conversation. The flavours are complemented by a final platter of grapes, figs, dates and nuts dipped in honey—thyme honey, if possible.

GREEK GRILL

> *The meze platter features sweet and savoury nibbles to be enjoyed with Retzina.*

I love this type of menu because the guest list can be doubled without doubling my work. I simply buy more dips, olives, fruits and nuts and have these additional items ready in the kitchen to refresh the platters as the night progresses. There will be more food to grill, but fortunately this is a type of cooking that does not require me to interrupt my conversation. My outdoor parties often revolve around the grill. Everyone seems to be an expert, so once my friends start telling me the best way to grill, I let them take over.

Two dips, hummus and tzatziki, accompany the grilled platter. Store-bought varieties are widely available, but if you have time and would prefer to offer homemade dips, here are two favourite recipes.

HUMMUS: In a food processor, combine 2 cups (500 mL) canned or cooked chickpeas, ⅔ cup (150 mL) tahini, 6 cloves garlic, 3 tbsp (45 mL) lemon juice, ½ cup (125 mL) plain yogurt, ¼ cup (50 mL) parsley and a pinch cayenne. Process the mixture until it is smooth.

TZATZIKI: Place 2 cups (500 mL) yogurt in cheesecloth or in a coffee filter over a container in the refrigerator; let drain at least 2 hours. Peel and remove seeds from 1 cucumber, grate and place in a fine sieve, cheesecloth or tea towel; squeeze out excess moisture.

Stir the cucumber into the thickened yogurt and add 2 tbsp (25 mL) lemon juice, 2 tbsp (25 mL) olive oil, 1 minced clove garlic, and ⅓ cup (75 mL) chopped mint or dill, or a mix.

Ouzo is the obvious choice for sipping in the garden, served in tall glasses with plenty of cold water. The meze tradition is designed for nibbling while you enjoy sparkling company and heady wine—thus keeping you from losing your head.

0:00 Have a sip of Retsina, an acquired taste ideal for this menu, if you appreciate the rough charms of this Greek wine.

0:01 *For the potato salad:* In a medium pot, cover the potatoes with cold salted water and bring them to a boil. Reduce the heat to simmer and cook them until they are fork tender, about 15 to 20 minutes; then rinse under cold running water.
For the calamari: Whisk together 3 tbsp (45 mL) olive oil, 3 tbsp (45 mL) lemon juice and chopped mint. Score the calamari by cutting horizontal slices halfway through the body so each piece consists of five or six attached rings. Toss them in the marinade and set aside.

0:10 Trim the dandelion, watercress and endive. Submerge them in a sink of cold water. Gently move the greens around to dislodge any dirt and grit, and then lift them out of water, leaving the dirt behind. Repeat in fresh water if necessary. Drain.

0:15 *To prepare the meze platter:* Cut the fennel bulb into thin wedges. Cut the tomato into four thick slices. Place the fennel and tomato in a bowl and add the artichokes. Toss with 2 tbsp (25 mL) olive oil, then season with salt and pepper to taste. Place an additional 2 tbsp (25 mL) oil in a small bowl next to grill for basting. Place the fennel mixture and pita on a tray near the grill. A hot grill will be required 30 minutes from now; preheat as necessary. Prepare a platter for the grilled foods with a bed of mint sprigs, lemon wedges and hot peppers.

0:25 *To prepare fruits and nuts:* Place honey in a dipping bowl and set on tray; surround the bowl with grapes, figs, dates, walnuts and almonds.

0:32 *To prepare the accompaniments:* Using either a tray with several compartments or a platter with three bowls, set out the hummus (reserve 2 tbsp/25 mL for the salad dressing) and sprinkle paprika over top. Place the tzatziki in another bowl and garnish with mint sprigs. In the third bowl, combine the green and kalamata olives.

0:40 In a large salad bowl, place 3 tbsp (45 mL) lemon juice and stir in ½ tsp (2 mL) salt until dissolved. Whisk in 2 tbsp (25 mL) hummus and the olive oil. Cut or tear greens into bite-size pieces, place them in bowl, sprinkle them with additional salt to cut any bitterness and toss in the dressing. Halve the potatoes and place them around the

circumference of bowl. Crumble feta cheese on top of the salad.

0:50 Place calamari, tomato, fennel and artichokes on a medium-hot grill. Cook 3 minutes on each side. Baste with the remaining olive oil. If you do not have room to grill everything at once, cook the vegetables first, then the calamari. Transfer them to prepared platter. Brush the pita with olive oil and warm them on the grill, 1 minute on each side. Cut into wedges and serve with dips.

Grilled Meze Platter

7 tbsp (100 mL) olive oil
3 tbsp (45 mL) lemon juice
1 tbsp (15 mL) chopped mint
8 pieces cleaned calamari (about 1¾ lb/875 g), tentacles removed
1 bulb fennel
1 large green tomato
1 can (14 oz/398 mL) whole artichoke hearts, drained
Sea salt and fresh pepper
4 to 6 pieces pita bread
Mint sprigs
2 lemons, cut into wedges
4 hot red peppers

Accompaniments

1 cup (250 mL) hummus (store-bought or homemade)
½ tsp (2 mL) sweet paprika
1 cup (250 mL) tzatziki (store-bought or homemade)
Mint sprigs
½ cup (125 mL) each green olives and kalamata olives (see Marinated Mushrooms and Olives, page 76)

New Potato Salad with Wild Greens

12 mini new potatoes
4 heads baby dandelion greens
1 bunch watercress
½ bunch curly endive
3 tbsp (45 mL) lemon juice
½ tsp (2 mL) sea salt
2 tbsp (25 mL) hummus
3 tbsp (45 mL) olive oil, preferably Greek
3 oz (90 g) feta cheese

Honey-Dipped Fruits and Nuts

¼ cup (50 mL) thyme honey
1 bunch red grapes
4 fresh figs, halved
8 dates
2 oz (50 g) shelled walnut halves
2 oz (50 g) shelled almonds

MENU FOR TWO

Tomatoes with Red Onion and Parmesan

Prosciutto and Smoked Turkey Wraps

Carrot and Apple Salad

Lemon Cheesecake

When the weather is sizzling hot, any joy I have ever derived from my kitchen evaporates. I shun both stove and oven. I neither boil water nor make toast. At the same time, both my appetite and my culinary curiosity are excited by the wealth of fresh fruits and vegetables available, so I turn my imagination to devising menus that celebrate beautiful uncooked but well-prepared simple foods.

NO COOKING REQUIRED

Change into something comfortable, put on some music, open a window and hope for a soft breeze.

Everywhere there are abundant hues. Nature's palette is coloured by the healthy glow of red tomatoes, green cucumbers, vibrant peppers and earthy carrots. Leafy greens from spinach to Swiss chard lie in moist repose. It seems a sin to bend these stunning foods to my will by boiling, simmering, sautéing and frying them. Everything I need for a wonderful meal is offered in fresh raw fruits and vegetables, full of the vitamins and minerals usually lost in the cooking process.

In this menu, a simple appetizer shows off ripe field tomatoes, incontestably my favourite summer food. Every year I plant a tomato garden. When space has been limited, this garden has been one plant in a pot on the balcony, but other times I have had earth enough for more tomatoes than I could eat. Picking them from the vine and enjoying the fruit moments later, with nothing to mask their intense flavour but a little salt—this is heaven. (Never banish such tomatoes to the cold, dark refrigerator, where their flavour is dulled and the effect on their texture is unspeakable.)

This lemon cheesecake recipe requires no baking and sets in less than an hour. Whipped cream adds structure and contributes to the light texture. Chocolate curls poised on top of almost any dessert add a professional-looking touch. Pastry chefs shave large curls from blocks of couverture ("covering"), a chocolate used for moulding and dipping. If you are unable to locate couverture, a thick, flat bar of good milk or white chocolate works best for making curls. (Dark chocolate crumbles more easily.)

A full-bodied white wine with some complexity is needed for this meal and a good California Chardonnay, with minimal oak, fits the bill exactly. Balsamic vinegar is always a tough match because of its acidity, so consider sparkling water for the appetizer course.

When you can't stand the heat, get out of the kitchen and into the garden, with this cool midsummer night's dream of a menu.

0:00 Change into something really comfortable and put on some cool music—Quincy Jones or maybe Erykah Badu. Open a window and hope for a soft summer breeze.

0:01 *To make the cheesecake:* In a bowl, whip the cream until it is semi-firm. Add the sugar and continue to whip until stiff peaks form. Set aside. In another bowl, whip together the cream cheese, lemon juice and vanilla until the mixture is very smooth. Fold in the whipped cream. Spoon it into chocolate dessert shells, if you're using them, or individual bowls. Rub your hands over the chocolate bar to warm it, then run a chef's knife (a large unserrated knife) down the back of the chocolate bar to shave off curls. Stand the curls vertically in centre of cheesecake. Place the cake in the refrigerator.

0:15 *For the dip:* In a ramekin, combine the lemon and lime juices; with a fork, whisk in the mustard. Stir in basil and salt. This sharp dip is served with the main course wraps.

0:20 *To make wraps:* If using a whole turkey breast, cut the meat into four large batons (about 5 inches/12.5 cm long and ¼ inch/6 mm wide). Cut the red pepper lengthwise into eight batons. Briefly soak one rice roll wrapper in warm water until it is pliable and soft. (If it sits in the water for too long, it will fall apart.) Lie the wrapper on a flat surface. Fold the top over 1 ½ inches (3.5 cm) to make a straight edge. Layer the ingredients in the centre of the wrapper so they protrude 1 inch (2.5 cm) from the top in the following order: one piece prosciutto, one lettuce leaf, one basil leaf, one turkey baton or slice, and two red pepper batons. Fold the left edge of the rice wrapper over the ingredients and tuck it under them. Next, fold the bottom of wrap over the ingredients. Then roll the whole thing from left to right until the ingredients are snugly wrapped. Repeat for the remaining rolls; place two on each dinner plate. Cover with plastic and refrigerate until you are ready to serve them.

0:40 *For the carrot and apple salad:* Peel and grate the carrot and apple into a mixing bowl. Add mayonnaise, raisins and coriander. Toss to combine them. Add salt and pepper to taste. Spoon the salad onto the dinner plates, next to the rolls. Refrigerate until serving.

0:50 *For tomatoes:* Slice the tomatoes ⅓-inch (8-mm) thick and arrange overlapping slices on two salad plates. Scatter onion rings over each plate. Sprinkle on salt and pepper to taste. Drizzle with olive oil, then balsamic vinegar. Use a vegetable peeler or knife to shave fresh parmesan over tomatoes. Serve.

Tomatoes with Red Onion and Parmesan

2 ripe field tomatoes
¼ red onion, sliced in thin rings
Sea salt and fresh pepper
2 tbsp (25 mL) extra virgin olive oil
2 tsp (10 mL) balsamic vinegar
1 oz (30 g) parmesan (ungrated)

Prosciutto and Smoked Turkey Wraps

2 oz (60 g) smoked turkey breast, whole or sliced
½ red pepper
4 rice roll wrappers
4 very thin slices prosciutto
4 small leaves red leaf lettuce
4 leaves basil

Citrus and Mustard Dip

2 tbsp (25 mL) lemon juice
1 tbsp (15 mL) lime juice
1 tsp (5 mL) Dijon mustard
2 small leaves basil, sliced thinly
Pinch sea salt

Carrot and Apple Salad

1 large carrot
1 golden delicious apple
2 tbsp (25 mL) mayonnaise
2 tbsp (25 mL) raisins
1 tbsp (15 mL) chopped coriander
Sea salt and fresh pepper

Lemon Cheesecake

¼ cup (50 mL) whipping cream
2 tbsp (25 mL) granulated sugar
3 oz (90 g) cream cheese
1 tbsp (15 mL) lemon juice
1 tsp (5 mL) pure vanilla extract
2 3-inch (7.5-cm) chocolate dessert shells, optional
1 thick, flat milk chocolate bar

MENU FOR TWO

Peperonata

Grilled New York Strip Loin
in Herbed Butter

Potato Coins and Field
Tomatoes

Grilled Plums in Golden Syrup

Summer's here and the time is right for grilling in the backyard. Writing for a magazine necessitates that I produce my column several months ahead of time so it can go through all the many stages of production prior to publication. The result is that when the time comes for me to write my summer pieces, I am usually knee deep in snow while my neighbours wonder why I have chosen such a cold day in February to have a barbecue. Since I'm writing this for the book, my more leisurely schedule allowed for the pleasure of actually cooking this meal on a hot, sunny August day. I was also able to make use of the seasonal bounty of local fresh peppers and plums, as well as herbs from my garden.

IT'S GRILLING TIME AGAIN

Peperonata is often served with onions and tomatoes, but the first course presented here is splendid in its simplicity.

The first course is a simplified version of an Italian dish. Peperonata is often served with onions and tomatoes but the first course presented here is splendid in its purity. Sweet peppers in season, roasted on the barbecue and served with a drizzle of extra virgin olive oil, a little garlic and a pinch of salt and pepper really need nothing more to delight the senses. At this time of year, when peppers in all their many colours are readily available and comparatively inexpensive, I often buy them by the bushel full. Once they're roasted, I store them in olive oil in the fridge and use them to brighten up salads, sandwiches and pastas. A favourite sandwich at our house is roasted peppers, chèvre and aioli on crusty Calabrese bread.

One rarely sees a porterhouse steak anymore. People are reluctant to sit down to something quite that large in these fat-conscious days. But subtract the tenderloin and you have the new king of the red-meat circuit: the New York strip. This tender cut is ideal for quick grilling; marinating can do great things for the flavour but is not necessary for

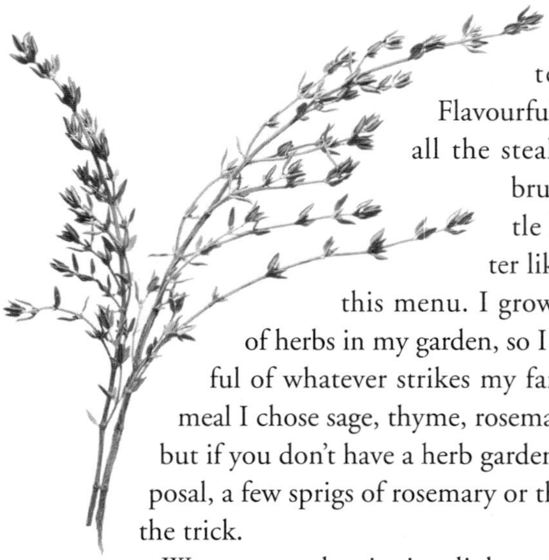

tenderizing. Flavourful on its own, all the steak needs is a brush with a little herbed butter like the one in this menu. I grow all manner of herbs in my garden, so I take a handful of whatever strikes my fancy. For this meal I chose sage, thyme, rosemary and basil, but if you don't have a herb garden at your disposal, a few sprigs of rosemary or thyme will do the trick.

Warmer weather invites lighter desserts, so I offer here an uncomplicated, grilled plum with golden syrup. When writing *Recipes for Homemade Love,* I was introduced to Tate & Lyle's Golden Syrup. This cane syrup has such a pure rich taste that I now use it alone for a quick sauce for all types of desserts from pastry to custard.

An Italian Cabernet Sauvignon is an ideal choice for this menu, complementing both the smoky flavour of the grilled foods and the heritage of our peperonata.

0:00 Ladies and gentlemen, start your barbecues. You will want a medium high heat.

0:01 *For the peperonata:* Place the peppers on barbecue. Cook each side until the skin is blistering, about 5 minutes per side. When they are finished, transfer them to a bowl, cover it with plastic wrap and set it aside.

For the vegetables: Wash the potato and cut it into ¼-inch (6-mm) coins. In a pot, cover the potatoes with cold, salted water and bring it to a boil. Let boil until the potatoes are three quarters cooked, 10 to 12 minutes. Cut the tomato in half horizontally.

0:15 *For the herbed butter:* Chop the herbs and stir them into the butter. Place the mixture in a container on or near the grill to melt. Assemble the vegetables, steak and utensils, and bring them to the grill.

0:20 Peel the peppers and arrange the flesh in a tricoloured fan design on two plates. Thinly slice the garlic and place the slices on the peppers. Drizzle olive oil on top and salt and pepper to taste. Garnish with basil leaves.

0:30 *To grill the steak and vegetables:* Brush butter on each steak and all the vegetables; salt and pepper the steak and potatoes, and set it all on the grill. Place the tomato halves cut side up. Cook the potato coins till they are golden with dark grill lines on both sides, then set them on the warming rack. If your grill doesn't have a warming rack, place them in a covered bowl or in a warm, not hot, oven, taking care that they don't dry out. Cook the tomatoes until the juices begin to come to the surface, then turn them and grill the top side for 3 to 4 minutes, until the tops are seared but not mushy. Turn them again and grill them until they are cooked but not falling apart, about 5 minutes; when they're done, set them on the warming rack. Sear each steak on one side for 4 to 5 minutes, then turn it and sear the other side. Cook steaks till they reach the

desired doneness, turning twice more and brushing liberally with herbed butter.

0:55 Cut the plums into quarters and set them near grill. They will take 5 minutes to grill so you can either cook them now and set them aside until the dessert course or grill them just before service. Simply set them, skin side down, on the grill over a medium heat until they are hot throughout. Serve the quarters in a flower pattern with syrup drizzled on top.

Peperonata

3 peppers, one red, one yellow, one orange
1 clove garlic
1 tbsp (15 mL) extra virgin olive oil
Sea salt and fresh pepper
6 leaves basil

New York Strip Loin in Herbed Butter

1 sprig rosemary
1 sprig thyme
2 leaves basil
2 leaves sage
2 tbsp (25 mL) butter
2 8-oz (250 g) strip loins
Sea salt and fresh pepper

Potato Coins and Field Tomatoes

1 large Yukon gold potato
1 large field tomato

Grilled Plums in Golden Syrup

2 large plums
2 tsp (10 mL) golden cane or corn syrup

MENU FOR TWO

Mixed Grain Salad

Skewered Capon Breasts

Grilled Vegetables

Gingered Cherries Jubilee

Almost every culture has a culinary history that embraces barbecuing. Even before human beings figured out how to control fire, they grilled their meat using whatever means nature was kind—or cruel—enough to provide. As different cultures evolved, each refined grilling techniques in its own fashion: Greece's classical hero Odysseus feasted on flame-roasted meat when he wasn't outwitting a cyclops or playing hostage to Circe; in the upper reaches of Mongolia, Genghis Khan fed his armies on spit-roasted meat; and farther east the Sumatrans perfected the art of grilling over a fire of coconut shells. The origins of the word "barbecue" are nearly as international as the method itself. Most likely the term came from indigenous peoples of Hispaniola in the Caribbean who called their green-wood lattice grills *barbacoa* and named their cooking method *boucan,* which was really more of a smoking method. They taught this technique to a motley crew of European outcasts, runaways and pirates who had settled there. When the marauding bunch took to the high seas, they took with them the boucan method and soon became known as *boucaniers* to the French and buccaneers to the English.

UNIVERSAL GRILL

The people of Hispaniola taught their "barbacoa" technique to a motley crew of European outcasts, runaways and pirates.

The Spanish take credit for adapting the word *barbacoa* to "barbecue" and importing the term and technique to Mexico and the southern United States. A competing theory relates "barbecue" back to the French term for spit-roasting a whole animal *barbe à queue* (beard to tail). My own favourite interpretation comes from Pedro Guanikeyu Torres, tribal council elder of the Taino people, who informs us that the Taino word *barbicu,* which is probably cognate with *barbacoa,* means the "sacred fire pit."

Like the barbecue itself, this month's flavours are a salute to global cuisine. Our barbecue dinner takes tried-and-true North American favourites, such as grilled capon and cherries jubilee, and gives them an international twist. The capon (larger but more tender than most chicken) is dressed with coriander and brushed with Japanese rice wine (sake) and ketjap manis, a sweet Indonesian soy sauce. The jubilee is spiced with crystallized ginger. In keeping with this international theme, Asian eggplant, Italian radicchio and zucchini accompany the capon on the grill, and the couscous salad has North African roots.

When you are cooking outdoors, keep your drink choices simple and let them reflect the meal's casual mood. An Asian beer will help cool your thirst at the grill. Clean-flavoured sake can be warmed up in a bain marie and served in small cups on a cool summer night. If wine is a must, avoid reds—soy, ginger and coriander will leave you tasting the tannin. Instead, opt for a dry Riesling or Sauvignon Blanc.

0:00 You will need a steady, medium heat 40 minutes from now, so start your barbecue whenever appropriate.

0:01 In a small bowl, combine the sake with ketjap manis, 2 tsp (10 mL) sugar and ¼ tsp (1 mL) sea salt. Slide a sharp, thin knife horizontally through the thickest part of each breast. Cut two skewers from sugarcane (each about ¾ inch/2 cm thick). Push a skewer through the cut made in each breast. Mince the garlic and combine it with the coriander. Using your fingers, stuff half the mixture under each capon skin. Brush with marinade and set the capon aside.

0:15 Cut the radicchio into 2-inch (5-cm) wedges, halve the eggplants lengthwise and cut both zucchini lengthwise into ½-inch (1-cm) thick strips. Set vegetables on platter. In a small bowl, mix lemon juice and sea salt; whisk in ¼ cup (50 mL) oil; brush the vegetables with this mixture. Add pepper to taste. Set vegetables aside.

0:20 Boil 1 cup (250 mL) water in a saucepan and at least ½ cup (125 mL) water in a kettle. While the water is coming to a boil, finely dice the onion and cucumber. Rinse the pea sprouts and set them aside to dry. Place the couscous in a mixing bowl. Pour ½ cup (125 mL) boiling water from the kettle into a measuring cup and mix with ¼ tsp (1 mL) sea salt and 1 tsp (5 mL) olive oil. Pour liquid over the couscous and stir until the liquid is mostly absorbed. Cover the bowl with a damp cloth and set it aside. Stir the bulgur into the boiling water on the stove. Simmer for 10 minutes or until the grains have absorbed the water. While the bulgur is cooking, whisk together the balsamic vinegar, soy sauce, sugar and ¼ cup (50 mL) oil. Remove the bulgur from heat and cover with a damp cloth.

0:35 Wash and pit the cherries; chop the crystallized ginger. In a saucepan, combine the cherries, ginger and jelly; set the pan aside near the stove.

0:40 Place the capon halves on the grill, skin side down, over a moderate heat. Do not allow the barbecue to flame or the capon and sugarcane will burn. Occasionally brush the capon generously with the marinade. Turn the skewers every 5 minutes, or sooner if flare-ups are frequent. The capon will take about 20 minutes to cook. To test for doneness, press into the thickest part with your finger; it will be very firm when done.

0:45 While the capon cooks, fluff the couscous with a fork until each grain is separate—don't leave any clumps. In a salad bowl, mix the couscous with the bulgur, red onion and cucumber. Toss with the dressing. Add the pea sprouts last. Garnish with more pea sprouts or cucumber, if desired.

0:50 Add the brushed vegetables to the grill; cook each side 3 to 5 minutes until it is tender.

0:60 When the vegetables and capon are done, turn off the barbecue and serve everything at once on festive platters for a casual, relaxed presentation.

When the time comes for dessert, stir the brandy and kirsch into cherry mixture and gently heat the mixture until it is just warm—don't cook off the alcohol; flambé by touching with a lit match. Pour, while warm, over two bowls of vanilla ice cream.

Mixed Grain Salad

1 ½ cups (375 mL) water
½ small red onion
½ English cucumber
1 cup (250 mL) pea sprouts
½ cup (125 mL) couscous
¼ tsp (1 mL) sea salt
¼ cup (50 mL) plus 1 tsp (5 mL) olive oil
½ cup (125 mL) bulgur
1 tbsp (25 mL) balsamic vinegar
½ tsp (2 mL) soy sauce
¼ tsp (1 mL) granulated sugar

Skewered Capon Breasts

¼ cup (50 mL) sake
¼ cup (50 mL) ketjap manis or 2 tbsp (25 mL) soy sauce mixed with 2 tbsp (25 mL) molasses
2 tsp (10 mL) granulated sugar
¼ tsp (1 mL) sea salt
2 boneless capon breast halves, skin on
1 piece (6 to 8 in/15 to 20 cm) fresh or canned sugarcane
2 cloves garlic
¼ cup (50 mL) chopped coriander

Grilled Vegetables

½ head radicchio
2 Asian eggplants
1 green zucchini
1 yellow zucchini
2 tbsp (25 mL) lemon juice
⅛ tsp (0.5 mL) sea salt
¼ cup (50 mL) olive oil
Pepper

Gingered Cherries Jubilee

1 cup (250 mL) fresh cherries
¼ cup (50 mL) crystallized ginger
2 tbsp (25 mL) cherry jelly or redcurrant jelly
¼ cup (50 mL) brandy
2 tbsp (25 mL) kirsch
2 cups (500 mL) vanilla ice cream

MENU FOR FOUR

Warm Marinated Mushrooms
and Olives

Grilled Jumbo Shrimp with Fresh
Peach and Cilantro Salsa

Fresh Corn in Husks

Grilled Pineapple with
Lemon Sorbet

What better accompaniment to fine food than a good story. Myths and legends told since antiquity comfort the psyche and warm the soul, much like a good soup. A favourite pastime of mine is to seek out stories from ancient civilizations. As these fables tell of the creation of the universe, the birth of humanity and the laws of society, so too do they speak of the origin of many foods.

MYTHIC FOOD

Myths and legends speak of the origin of many foods.

To begin a meal with olives is said to invite peace and harmony to the table. The olive tree has been sacred since the first one grew near the Mediterranean thousands of years ago. According to Greek mythology, when the world was young, there were 12 great Olympians, including Athena who was born out of the head of Zeus. She was the goddess of wisdom, and her uncle was Poseidon, the god of the sea (a randy old god, but that's another story). There was a great contest between the two for the city of Athens, the centre of ancient Greek culture. Both gods stood atop the Acropolis and vied to bestow the greatest gift upon the city. Poseidon caused an immense spring to burst forth, which looked wonderful but because it gushed salt water was not really practical. Form over function just didn't cut the mustard. Athena won the contest by producing the olive tree and teaching the people of Athens to cultivate and use it for food, oil and wood.

Searching out the myth behind the origin of corn brings us to another time, another place. One of the greatest gods in Aztec lore is Quetzalcoatl. From the creation of the sun, the earth and the heavens to the naming of the land and the sea, Quetzalcoatl is a unifying presence. He was at once powerful and fun, encouraging drunkenness, fertility, music and dance. His great contributions to humanity include the gifts of fire, domesticating animals and, perhaps the greatest gift of all, the discovery of maize. Maize is, of course, corn, and is at the heart of Mexican cuisine.

From China we have the tale of the deity Shou-xing, whose name means "Star of Longevity." Shou-xing is generally portrayed holding a peach, which represents longevity, and his symbol is the mushroom. As a child, he visited the God of the North Pole and the God of the South Pole, bringing them food and wine and remaining silent in their presence. For his trouble and his quiet demeanour, they rewarded him by granting him long life. The moral of this story: never pass up an opportunity to keep your mouth closed and never underestimate the power of hospitality.

This menu contains ingredients from all of these myths: olives and mushrooms in the appetizer, peaches in the salsa for the shrimp and corn to accompany the main course. It is fitting that this is a barbecue. Cooking these ancient foods out of doors, over an open fire, is further reminder of times long past, when humanity was young, the world was new and everyone loved a good cookout.

CATHERINE'S WINE TIP

To enjoy with this menu, our modern, feminine Bacchus suggests a New Zealand Sauvignon Blanc. This crisp, clear New World wine carries a little more weight than an Old World Sauvignon Blanc, and suits the sharp, fresh flavours of the meal.

0:00 Take a moment to remember Athena, Quetzalcoatl and Shou-xing and everything they have done for modern cuisine. Prepare the grill; an even, medium high heat will be required.

0:01 Remove the corn silk and soak the cobs in cold water so the husks won't burn.

0:05 *To prepare the mushrooms:* Wash the mushrooms and pat them dry, then remove the stems. Peel the pearl onions and smash the garlic cloves to remove their skin. Peel the shallot and cut it into thin rings. Roughly chop the herbs. Heat the oil in a small pan over a low to medium heat. (This can be done on the stove or by placing the pan over a warm spot on the barbecue, but the pan will suffer a little smoking by the barbecue.) Add these ingredients along with the olives to the warm oil and let the flavours slowly infuse until you are ready to serve them. The intention is not to fry, but to warm the mushrooms and olives gently, so temper the heat accordingly. Serve them drizzled with warm oil and top with shaved parmesan.

0:20 *For the shrimp:* Remove the shells from shrimp, leaving the tails attached. Cover the shrimp in olive oil and lightly season them with salt and pepper. Put them aside in refrigerator until you are ready to cook them. Peel the peach and cut it into ¼-inch (6-mm) cubes. Cut the onion into small dice and chop the coriander. Mix the peaches, onion, coriander and sesame oil, and set the mixture aside until it's time to serve it.

0:40 *To grill the corn:* After soaking the cobs, gently peel back the husks—do not remove them. Rub butter into the corn and season with salt and pepper. Cover the cobs again with their husks and place them on the barbecue to cook, turning them occasionally for 10 to 15 minutes or until the corn is hot throughout.

0:50 *To prepare the pineapple:* Cut two 1-inch (2.5-cm) rounds from the pineapple, leaving the skin on. Rub both sides with oil and lightly sprinkle them with salt. During dinner, grill the rounds until they are well browned, about 10 to 12 minutes on each side. Keep them warm. To serve, cut each round in half to make two semicircles. Cut the other halves into four wedges. On each plate, prop up the semicircle with one of the wedges, place the sorbet partially on the semicircle and garnish with the remaining wedges.

After the appetizer: The shrimp will taste best if it is grilled just before service. Place them on a medium hot barbecue and grill for about 3 minutes on each side, or until the flesh is pink on the outside and white on the inside. Serve with the salsa and corn.

Warm Marinated Mushrooms and Olives

10 small mushrooms, button or crimini, about 3 oz (90 g)
6 pearl onions
2 cloves garlic
1 small shallot
3 leaves basil
4 stems thyme
¼ cup (50 mL) extra virgin olive oil
8 large green olives
1 oz (30 g) fresh parmesan

Grilled Jumbo Shrimp with Fresh Peach and Cilantro Salsa

1 lb (500 g) jumbo shrimp (6 to 10)
1 tbsp (15 mL) olive oil
Sea salt and fresh pepper
1 peach
2 tbsp (25 mL) chopped red onion
2 tbsp (25 mL) chopped fresh coriander
2 tbsp (25 mL) sesame oil

Fresh Corn in Husks

2 corn cobs in husks
2 tsp (10 mL) butter
Sea salt and fresh pepper

Grilled Pineapple with Lemon Sorbet

¼ pineapple
2 tbsp (25 mL) olive oil
Sea salt
1 cup (250 mL) lemon sorbet

MENU FOR TWO

Gazpacho

Muffuletta

Dandelion and Pasta Salad

Fresh Fruit and Biscotti

Packing a proper picnic basket can be a work of art. In the fine weather, I often assemble a very utilitarian basket before leaving the house in the morning so my son and I can spend the day outdoors without having to worry about where to stop for lunch. For this, I have an insulated bag with many sizes of sealable plastic containers. We also take along a compact picnic set with colourful and durable plastic plates, cups and cutlery. This complement is basic and useful and I don't worry too much about losing any of the pieces. We have a large, faded Mickey Mouse blanket, too, for getting comfortable

DANDELION WHINE

Packing a picnic should be a work of art.

Then there are the picnics that resemble a Victorian outing. I dust off my large wicker basket with its many trays, shine the silver cutlery and carefully pack the crystal stemware. The linens are ironed and I even pack a small vase for flowers. These picnics can become delightfully complicated and must be planned days in advance. Formal picnics are really a practice more suited to those with the time available to the idle rich of yesteryear; still I enjoy planning at least one elegant outing a season.

For days when it makes such good sense to abandon the kitchen, store-bought tapenade and roasted peppers are perfectly acceptable convenience foods. For my recipe for homemade tapenade, see page 17. The simplest method I have found for ROASTING PEPPERS is to place them directly on the middle rack of a 450°F (230°C) oven, until the skin is browned and bubbling on all sides. It makes less mess if you place a tray on the bottom rack of the oven to catch any juices. Remove the peppers from the oven and place them in a stainless steel bowl, then tightly cover the bowl with plastic wrap. When the peppers have cooled, the skin peels off easily. There are those who say that peppers need to be blackened over an open flame, and certainly this method yields a sweet, rich, roasted pepper. I, however, opt for the easier, neater method described here, with totally satisfactory results.

Stefanie Killen, pastry chef for Toronto's Senator Restaurant, has been generous enough to share one of her sinful and sweet recipes with me. This biscotti is a hit and while there is not time to prepare it in the 60 minutes allotted, I present the recipe here for when there is time to tinker in your own pastry kitchen. This recipe makes a dozen cookies, enough for three picnics.

Biscotti Put ½ cup (125 mL) soft butter in a bowl with 1¾ cups (425 mL) brown sugar and beat with an electric mixer until the mixture is soft and fluffy. Add one egg and mix, then add a second egg and stir until it is well mixed. With a spoon or a spatula, stir in 2¼ cups (625 mL) whole almonds and ½ cup (125 mL) each of chopped dark, milk and white chocolate. Sift together 2½ cups (625 mL) all-purpose flour and ½ tsp (2 mL) baking powder and gradually fold them into the other mixture until they are just incorporated. Divide the dough into two equal-sized pieces and shape each into a log about 2 inches (5 cm) wide and the length of your baking tray. Line the tray with parchment paper and bake the logs at 350°F (180°C) for 15 to 20 minutes or until they are golden brown. Let them cool for 10 minutes, then slice, while they are still warm, into 10 cookies per log. Lay the biscotti back on the tray and return to a 325°F (160°C) oven for an additional 10 to 15 minutes. Let them cool, then store them in an airtight container for up to 3 weeks.

While wine is suitable for drinking at a picnic in your own yard, in Canada we have some rather unsophisticated laws about quaffing in the park. There are, however, a number of fantastic alcohol-free beverages, ideally suited for bringing along to public places. My favourite is an Elderflower Pressé; with its refreshing character and charming bouquet, it is almost as pleasant as drinking a light Pinot Gris.

CATHERINE'S WINE TIP

With gazpacho I love a Tio Pepe or Dry Sac sherry. For the main course, I would choose a chilled, dry Bordeaux, such as a Château Bonnet or Entre-de-Mers.

0:00 Assemble first the necessary accoutrements for your picnic basket. Will it be silver or plastic today?

0:01 Put 4 cups (1 L) salted water on to boil for the pasta.

To prepare the gazpacho: Cut the tomato into large wedges, cube the cucumber, dice the peppers, chop the onion and herbs, and mince the garlic. Combine all in the bowl of a food processor with the olive oil, juice and salt. Pulse until the vegetables are finely diced and liquid is emulsified. Do not blend or over-mix or the texture will be mushy. Put the mixture in the refrigerator to chill until you are ready to pack. Then place it in a thermos and serve in large cups.

0:15 *For the salad:* Cook the pasta in boiling water until it is tender but firm to the bite, about 5 to 7 minutes. Drain and rinse it with cold water. In a stainless steel bowl, whisk the lemon juice and salt until the salt is fully dissolved. Whisk in the olive oil and pesto until they are emulsified. Toss the pasta in the dressing. Wash

and pat dry the dandelion leaves. Place them in the bottom of a flat container and cover with pasta and dressing. Sprinkle walnuts over top. Cover and add the container to the picnic basket.

0:30 *To assemble the muffuletta:* Cut the bread horizontally through the centre to yield two even-sized discs. Chop the green olives and sundried tomatoes and combine them with the tapenade and olive oil. Spread the mixture over the inside of both pieces of bread. Layer smoked meat, provolone cheese, peppers and lettuce on one piece and cover with the other. Cut into two, wrap each and place them in picnic basket.

0:45 Wash the fruits and pat them dry. Cut the pears into thick wedges, toss them in a little lemon juice and seal them in a container. Pack the grapes and peaches loosely, as they are to be eaten by hand. Whether you have bought biscotti or made them from Stefanie's wonderful recipe, add them to the basket. And you're off!

Gazpacho

1 large tomato
⅓ English cucumber
¼ red pepper
¼ green pepper
1 spring onion
1 tbsp (15 mL) fresh oregano
1 tbsp (15 mL) fresh basil
1 clove garlic
3 tbsp (45 mL) olive oil
¼ cup (50 mL) V-8 juice
¼ tsp (1 mL) salt

Muffuletta

1 small loaf focaccia or other round bread, large enough for two hearty sandwiches
¼ cup (50 mL) pitted green olives
2 tbsp (25 mL) sundried tomatoes, softened or in oil
¼ cup (50 mL) tapenade
2 tbsp (25 mL) olive oil
5 oz (140 g) Montreal smoked meat
4 oz (120 g) provolone, sliced
6 oz (170 g) roasted red peppers
4 leaves lettuce

Dandelion and Pasta Salad

½ cup (125 mL) tubetti or other small pasta
1 tbsp (15 mL) lemon juice
¼ tsp (1 mL) salt
2 tbsp (25 mL) olive oil
1 tbsp (15 mL) pesto
8 to 10 leaves dandelion greens
2 tbsp (25 mL) crushed walnuts

Fresh Fruit and Biscotti

2 pears
Lemon juice
1 bunch grapes
1 peach
4 biscotti

MENU FOR TWO

Cream Cheese and
Avocado Roll-Ups

Roasted Chicken

White Bean Salad

Gingered Apricot Drops

I am writing this on a cold, rainy December day and the idea of a picnic is so delicious, I could cry. The closest I will come to dining alfresco for the next five months will be eating roasted cashews while waiting for the bus. Or perhaps an elegant luncheon in a solarium. A note: People who eat in glass restaurants shouldn't throw stones; it's impolite. And even the most charming and well-tended restaurant garden cannot compete with the unabashed joy of spreading a blanket in the shade of a great maple for a languorous early-evening picnic.

WRAP, DROP AND ROLL

Gingered Apricot Drops, a no-bake classic, is perfect for making on a sweltering summer day.

Wraps are all the rage for casual dining. A wide variety of flatbreads are now commonly available and are fantastic for a light sandwich. I like the sundried tomato and the pesto flavoured breads, more for their colour than their taste, as they make a charming package for an array of fillings. For this menu I have used cream cheese, avocado and alfalfa sprouts, but any foods that are suitable for a sandwich are ideal for wraps. Roasted chicken works wonderfully, as do deli meats and cheeses layered on the flatbread and then rolled. The wrap can be eaten whole or sliced on the diagonal to make an attractive display. To moisten the sandwich, cream cheese, mayonnaise dressing or a sour cream dip is spread first on the bread to keep the other ingredients in place and create a final seal after rolling.

More than just a pretty taste, navy beans are a valuable source of protein, iron and calcium, and they contain only a little more than 100 calories for a 1-cup (250-mL) serving. The salad in this menu combines these small white beans with fresh vegetables in a sharp shallot vinaigrette. The recipe is for a standard-sized can of beans, which will yield more salad than you are likely to eat. I never get around to using up partial cans of beans left over from recipes, so in this case, I prefer to make a larger salad; I purée the leftovers to make a white bean paste. The paste is tasty and convenient for spreading on toast or sandwiches and will keep, refrigerated, for 2 days.

High on my list of acceptable convenience foods is whole roasted or rotisserie chicken. At least once, and usually at mid week, I am in the position of needing to serve my family dinner in 60 seconds, never mind the luxury of 60 minutes. On these days, I feel perfectly comfortable presenting a store-bought bird with a big salad and some very good bread. Add some aged cheddar to the salad and all the food groups are represented, my family is comfortably fed and I can go back into my office to sweat out a deadline. However, when I do roast a chicken at home, I do it simply. The bird is washed and lightly salted inside and out, then sprinkled with the juice of one lemon. I stuff it with large pieces of onion and apple or garlic cloves, rub the outside with butter and liberally grind fresh pepper over the whole thing. I never bother to truss the bird, but place it in a shallow roasting pan, breast side up, and bake at 400°F (200°C) until the juices run clear. *The Joy of Cooking* suggests roasting the chicken on its side, turning it about a third of the way through cooking to roast on its other side, and then turning it breast side up for the last 15 to 30 minutes. This method does yield a somewhat moister breast and is worth trying when you're in the mood to fuss a bit over your fowl.

CATHERINE'S WINE TIP

Bring on the Valpolicella! It's a great wine to go with roasted chicken and white beans. For dessert, when dining at the home of my Italian mother-in-law, I bring a Moscato d'Asti and we follow this with a good strong espresso and shots of sambucca—si si!

Gingered Apricot Drops are based on the standard lemon drops grandma used to make. A classic no-bake cookie, they are perfect for a menu designed to be prepared without adding to the heat of your kitchen on a sweltering August day. (My December kingdom for a little sweltering!) The addition of ginger marmalade is my contribution to the standard, lending a slight bite to the drops. Ginger marmalade is a staple in my kitchen; I use it to glaze poultry (see the recipe for Cornish Hens on page 144) and fish, to flavour baked goods and to sweeten scones.

0:00 Go! Go outside while you still can move unfettered by rain and snow gear. Relish the absence of sleet, for soon enough you too will be confined to the long, dark Canadian winter.

0:01 *For apricot drops:* Using a knife or a food processor, dice the apricots as small as possible. Combine them in a bowl with the coconut and almonds. Stir in the marmalade, condensed milk and lemon extract. If the dough is too wet, add a little more diced apricots and almonds. Roll the dough into 1-inch (2.5-cm) balls and roll them in icing sugar. Refrigerate them until you are ready to pack the picnic basket; then place them in a container with a little extra icing sugar.

0:15 *To assemble the salad:* Drain and rinse the beans. Finely dice the cucumber, peppers and onion. In a large bowl, dissolve the salt in the vinegar and lemon. Whisk in the olive oil until the mixture is emulsified. Toss the beans and vegetables in dressing and place them in a sealable container for transport. Pack it in the picnic basket.

0:30 *To make the roll-ups:* Spread half the cream cheese over the entire surface of each tortilla. Cut the avocado into thin wedges and lay them in line in the centre of each tortilla. Gently rub the avocado with lemon. Lightly season the avocado with salt and pepper. Cover the avocado with alfalfa sprouts and roll up each tortilla. Wrap them tightly and refrigerate them until you are ready to pack.

0:45 When I buy a roasted chicken for a picnic, I prefer to pick it up on the way to the picnic so it is still warm when it is served. If time does not allow, keep the chicken refrigerated until you are ready to pack the basket, then pack it in an insulated bag with ice packs. Be sure to wrap it well so it is protected from dampness. To prepare the dip for the chicken, stir together the mustard and sour cream and refrigerate the mixture in a sealable container until you are ready to go.

TIP

Remember the golden rule of food safety: Keep hot foods hot and cold foods cold. Bacteria multiply quickly at temperatures between 40°F (4°C) and 140°F (60°C), so it is unwise to pack your picnic basket too early.

Cream Cheese and Avocado Roll-Ups

¼ cup (50 mL) cream cheese
2 7-inch (18-cm) plain or sundried tomato tortillas
1 avocado
2 lemon wedges
Sea salt and fresh pepper
½ cup (125 mL) alfalfa sprouts

Roasted Chicken

1 whole small roasted chicken
2 tbsp (25 mL) Dijon mustard
¼ cup (50 mL) sour cream

White Bean Salad

19 oz (540 mL) can navy beans
¼ English cucumber
¼ red pepper
¼ green pepper
1 green onion
2½ tbsp (35 mL) shallot vinegar
½ tsp (2 mL) sea salt
1 tsp (5 mL) lemon juice
⅓ cup (75 mL) extra virgin olive oil

Gingered Apricot Drops

2 tbsp (25 ml) dried apricots
⅔ cup (150 mL) shredded coconut
2 tbsp (25 ml) ground almonds
2 tbsp (25 ml) ginger marmalade
4 tbsp (60 mL) condensed milk
½ tsp (2 mL) lemon extract
1 tbsp (15 mL) icing sugar

F A L L

And so it happens that when I write of hunger,
I am really writing about love and the hunger for it,
and warmth and the love of it and the hunger for it …
and then the warmth and richness and fine reality
of hunger satisfied … and it is all one.

–*M.F.K. Fisher,* The Gastronomical Me

There's nothing more exciting to a good cook than the abundance of fresh, local produce available at harvest time. Fried green tomatoes, roasted vegetable pie, potato and garlic soup, apple crisp and port-poached pears are just some of the great dishes I love to make at this time of year.

Thanksgiving in our home has always been a celebration of family, friends and fine food. This section features family recipes for a crusted pork loin, watercress and roasted garlic soup and an uncomplicated apricot cake. Travelling further afield for inspiration, there's a holiday meal with a Latin beat. Ceviche is followed by a scaled-down version of mole, made simpler to accommodate our 60-minute theme. From Italy comes a meal centred on Cornish hens with a shallot and portobello mushroom sauce and finished with a dessert that would entice a goddess from her mother's home.

MENU FOR TWO

Céléri Rémoulade

T-bone Tails with
Peppercorn Sauce

Baked Potatoes

Spinach and
Mushroom-Stuffed Peppers

Poached Pears with Stilton

For inspiration this month, I look to that bastion of comfort and luxury, the great North American steakhouse. More popular now than ever, its resurgence reflects the inconsistency of the modern diet—Monday, granola and low-fat yogurt; Tuesday, vegetarian curry; and Wednesday, a big, juicy steak.

LUXURIOUS COMFORTS

Celeriac, or celery root, is often overlooked because of its daunting appearance.

At Hy's Encore steakhouse in Vancouver, the kitchen run by executive chef Wilson Lo cooks more than 1,000 steaks each week. Lo believes that dry aging is the secret to the perfect steak. In dry aging, the meat loses 40 to 60 percent of its mass through a loss of moisture and the dried and inedible outer layer, which is trimmed away. This effectively doubles the steak's price. For this reason, most commercial beef is wet aged inside vacuum-sealed plastic. Although dry aging is the best natural tenderizing technique, executive chef Frank Scordino of Toronto's Senator Steak House cautions that it is equally important to start with the finest beef and best cut you can muster.

The T-bone tails featured in this menu fit the bill perfectly, being the next best thing to tenderloin at less than one third of the price. The T-bone is tenderloin on one side of the bone and New York strip on the other. The tails come from New York strip, a tender cut of meat perfectly suited for quick cooking methods such as grilling or pan braising. The size of the pieces is somewhat irregular, but if you cook the strips whole and slice them on a sharp diagonal before serving, the medallions will be even. If you cannot find T-bone tails, New York strip is a good substitute.

A steakhouse that serves 1,000 steaks will undoubtedly serve 1,000 baked potatoes alongside them. Scordino suggests placing a large, washed russet potato on a bed of rock salt to bake. The rock salt will draw out moisture, producing a soft and fluffy texture within the potato.

Roasted red peppers have been a trendy restaurant food for more than a decade. For this meal, whole roasted peppers are stuffed with sautéed spinach and mushrooms, a harmony of flavours that looks stunning on the plate.

From escargots to filet mignon, steakhouses have always given more than a passing nod to classical French cuisine and I have followed suit by offering céléri rémoulade as an appetizer. Whether you call it céléri, celeriac or celery root, this vegetable's subtle and refreshing flavour is frequently overlooked because of its daunting appearance. Cut back the rough exterior, however, and you will be rewarded with a delicate-tasting treat. Celery root discolours quickly, so I dress it immediately after cutting or use lemon in the cooking water when preparing hot dishes.

This meal finishes with one of my personal favourites: port-poached pears with stilton and walnuts. A snap to prepare, this elegant dish is the perfect choice for the time-restricted cook.

0:00 Open the Merlot to let it breathe. Conduct a quality-control experiment.

0:01 Preheat oven to 400°F (200°C). Wash the potatoes and peppers.
To roast potatoes on a bed of rock salt: Put 2 cups (500 mL) rock salt in a shallow pan you don't mind scratching. Set the potatoes on the salt, then roast them in the oven. The rock salt can be used repeatedly. Or place potatoes directly on a baking sheet in the oven. Roast the peppers on a separate baking sheet. Take the steak out of refrigerator so it can come to room temperature.

0:05 In a small pot, bring port and water to a boil. Peel, core and halve the pears. Add the pears and cloves to the port, and reduce the heat to medium low. Simmer until the pears are tender but not mushy; the time will vary from 20 to 40 minutes, depending on the ripeness of the pears.

0:10 Chop 1½ tsp (7 mL) capers and whisk them together with the mayonnaise, anchovy paste and mustard. Coarsely grate the celery root, then the carrot; reserve the carrot for garnish. Stir the celery root into the mayonnaise mixture. Mould the rémoulade by stuffing half the mixture into a teacup; invert the cup and unmould the contents onto an appetizer plate. Repeat with a clean cup for the second plate. Garnish each with a ring of grated carrot and the remaining capers. Place the plates in the refrigerator to keep them cool until you are ready to serve them.

0:25 Wash the spinach and pat it dry with a cloth or paper towel. Wipe the mushrooms and halve any too large to serve whole. Heat 1 tbsp (15 mL) butter in a skillet over medium heat and sauté the spinach and mushrooms, about 5 minutes or until the mushrooms are lightly browned. Sprinkle them with salt and pepper to taste. Cover and set aside. Check the pears. When they are tender, remove them from the port mixture and place them on dessert plates. Refrigerate them to cool. Remove the cloves from the port mixture and, over medium heat, reduce the liquid to 2 tbsp (25 mL) syrup, stirring occasionally. (This will take 10 to 15 minutes.) When the syrup is fully reduced, use a rubber spatula to scrape the pot; drizzle the syrup over the pears.

0:45 Crush 1½ tsp (7 mL) green peppercorns with the flat side of a chef's knife or a rolling pin. Mix in a pinch of sea salt. Press the mixture onto both sides of the steaks. Remove the peppers from oven. Cover your hands with a cloth to protect your fingers and carefully peel the skin from the peppers, leaving the stems attached. Cut a slit in each pepper from top to bottom and gently scoop out the seeds with a small spoon. Drain off any liquid trapped inside the pepper and season the cavity lightly with salt and pepper to taste. Stuff the peppers with spinach and mushrooms and return them to the oven to keep warm.

0:60 Turn off the oven and prepare the steak: For well-done meat, begin cooking now; for rare or medium, serve céléri rémoulade and take a break between courses to prepare steak *à la minute.* Heat 1 tsp (5 mL) olive oil in an ovenproof skillet over medium high. Add 1 tsp (5 mL) butter. Sear the steak 2 minutes on each side. Remove it to a plate and let it rest, covered, in a warm spot. Reduce the heat to medium and pour the Merlot into the skillet to deglaze the pan by scraping any bits from the bottom with a wooden spoon—those bits enrich and flavour the sauce. Add 1½ tsp (7 mL) green peppercorns, stock and cream. Reduce mixture to 3 tbsp (45 mL) of smooth, velvety sauce. Stir frequently. For rare meat, serve immediately. For well-done steak, return it to the skillet with the sauce and place in oven to keep warm while the céléri rémoulade is served. If the juices from meat run into sauce, stir it.

To serve, cut the steak strips into medallions by slicing them on a steep diagonal; top with sauce. Cut the potatoes in half lengthwise and serve each with 1 tbsp (15 mL) sour cream and 2 whole chives. Place a stuffed pepper on each plate and serve.

Serve the pears garnished with stilton and walnuts. Some believe that an opened bottle of port is meant to be finished, but this may be excessive. Still, encourage your companion to linger over dessert with a glass of tawny and fine conversation.

Céléri Rémoulade

1 tbsp (15 mL) capers
¼ cup (50 mL) mayonnaise
½ tsp (2 mL) anchovy paste
½ tsp (2 mL) Dijon mustard
1 large or 2 small celery roots, peeled
1 large carrot, peeled

T-bone Tails with Peppercorn Sauce

1 tbsp (15 mL) green peppercorns
¾ lb (375 g) T-bone tails
Sea salt and fresh pepper
1 tsp (5 mL) olive oil
1 tsp (5 mL) butter
½ cup (125 mL) Merlot or another dry red wine
½ tsp (2 mL) concentrated beef stock
2 tbsp (25 mL) whipping cream

Baked Potatoes

2 russet potatoes
2 cups (500 mL) rock salt, optional
2 tbsp (25 mL) sour cream
4 chives

Spinach and Mushroom-Stuffed Peppers

2 red peppers, stems intact
2 cups (500 mL) spinach, lightly packed
1 cup (250 mL) small button mushrooms
1 tbsp (15 mL) butter
Sea salt and fresh pepper

Poached Pears with Stilton

1 cup (250 mL) port
1 cup (250 mL) water
2 firm, ripe, red Bartlett pears
2 whole cloves
2 to 3 oz (60 to 90 g) stilton
1 oz (30 g) freshly shelled walnut pieces

MENU FOR FOUR

Crudités with Tarragon Vinaigrette

Macaroni and Cheese or Sage Fusilli with Asiago

Peach Crumble

Given the choice of any food from life's great banquet, most children will opt for pizza. Because our son has two food professionals as parents, my husband and I expected him to naturally possess a palate superior to that of the average child. Wrong. I offer him filet mignon and he wants hot dogs. I cook coq au vin and he craves only chicken nuggets. I bake light-as-air pastry and he cries for doughnuts. And I, pressed for time, often find that my own dinner is dictated by his less-than-inspired tastes.

A FAMILY AFFAIR

Crudités, with a touch of tarragon vinaigrette, are a great starter for a family table.

It is, however, possible to prepare a meal that suits the taste buds of children and pleases adult palates. The trick, I have found, is to cook my child's favourite, then spice, season and alter the dish to suit my desire for more subtle and complex tastes.

Crudités are a great starter for the family table. Crunchy, raw vegetables go over much better with the tot and teen set than do eggplant caviar and mushroom croquettes—and they are so much easier to prepare. A tarragon vinaigrette adds a dash of sophistication for adults.

Macaroni and cheese heads up most children's top-ten lists and making it from scratch means you can turn the simple béchamel into something flavourful. A creamy, smooth and velvety sauce, béchamel is surprisingly easy to make, as long as you avoid the common pitfalls. Begin with a roux made of equal parts butter and flour. Cook it over a medium-high heat, stirring, until the flour begins to turn a light brown, imparting a pleasing, nutty undertone to the sauce. (Undercooked roux tastes floury.) Add cold liquid slowly to a hot roux to prevent lumps.

Canada's homegrown peaches are among the best in the world. Here, Toronto pastry chef Stefanie Killen shares a recipe for her favourite peach crumble.

Peaches and Late Harvest Riesling make the happiest of duets, while a light, crisp white wine with good acidity from northern Italy's Alto Adige will make the pasta course sing.

0:00 Wake up, hustle the kids off to school, go about your demanding day, run errands, buy groceries, fight the traffic home and, finally, put your feet up and relax. Just kidding. It's time to make dinner for four.

0:01 Preheat the oven to 375°F (190°C).
For macaroni: Place a large pot of salted water over high heat. Bring it to a boil.
Meanwhile, prepare the peach crumble: Blanch peaches by immersing them in boiling water for 30 seconds. Remove and briefly immerse them in ice water. Slip off the skins and cut the peaches into 1-inch (2.5-cm) slices. Place the slices in a bowl and toss them with lemon juice. In a separate bowl, stir together granulated sugar, 1 tsp (5 mL) flour and ginger. Add to the peaches and toss them to coat. Spread the mixture evenly in a 4-cup (1-L) baking dish or glass pie plate.
For the topping: Melt butter in a saucepan over low heat or in a covered dish in the microwave at medium for 1 to 2 minutes. In a bowl, combine ½ cup (125 mL) flour, oats, brown sugar and nutmeg. Drizzle melted butter over the mixture and lightly toss it with a fork until the ingredients are just combined. Sprinkle the topping over the peaches. Place the dish in the oven and set the timer for 30 to 35 minutes. When it is done, topping will be crisp and the filling bubbly.

0:20 *For macaroni:* Add macaroni to boiling water; stir to prevent sticking. Cook the pasta uncovered until it is firm but tender to the bite, about 10 minutes.
Meanwhile, make a roux: Melt butter in a saucepan over medium-high heat. Add flour, stirring with a wooden spoon until the mixture is lightly browned. Whisk in ⅓ cup (75 mL) milk until the mixture is smooth, then slowly whisk in the remaining milk. Cook, stirring, until the liquid is thick and creamy. Season it to taste with salt and pepper. Remove it from the heat and scoop out 1½ cups (375 mL) béchamel for macaroni and place it in a large bowl. Stir in the cheddar. (Leave the remaining sauce in the saucepan for the fusilli.)

0:30 Drain the macaroni, lightly salt it and toss it in the cheese sauce. Divide it between two individual casserole dishes; sprinkle both tops with bread crumbs. Place the dishes in the oven and set another timer for 25 minutes; the top will be lightly browned when the macaroni is done. (The macaroni is baked early so it cools to a child-friendly temperature before serving.)

0:35 *For the crudités:* Trim the green beans, radishes and onions. Remove the seeds from the red and yellow peppers; cut the peppers into thin sticks. Arrange the beans, radishes, onions, peppers, tomatoes and carrots on a platter. Pour vinegar into a small bowl and whisk in the sugar and salt until they are dissolved. Slowly whisk in the olive oil until it is emulsified. Place the bowl in the centre of a platter.

0:45 *For the fusilli:* Bring a large pot of salted water to a boil. Whisk white wine and cream into the reserved béchamel over a low heat. Roughly chop sundried tomatoes and sage; stir them into the sauce along with the nutmeg and cayenne. Add asiago. Cook the fusilli until it is firm but tender to the bite, about 10 minutes, while enjoying your crudités. Drain the cooked fusilli and briefly reheat the sauce. Lightly salt the fusilli, toss it with the asiago sauce and serve it immediately with freshly ground pepper and parmesan, if you're using it.

Crudités with Tarragon Vinaigrette

8 green beans
4 each radishes and green onions
1 each red pepper and yellow pepper
8 each cherry tomatoes and baby carrots
1 tbsp (15 mL) tarragon vinegar
¼ tsp (1 mL) granulated sugar
Pinch sea salt
3 tbsp (45 mL) olive oil

Macaroni and Cheese

¾ cup (175 mL) macaroni
3 tbsp (45 mL) butter
3 tbsp (45 mL) all-purpose flour
2 cups (500 mL) cold milk
Sea salt and fresh pepper
1 cup (250 mL) grated cheddar
1 tbsp (15 mL) dry bread crumbs

Sage Fusilli with Asiago

¼ cup (50 mL) whipping cream
¼ cup (50 mL) white wine
¾ cup (175 mL) reserved béchamel
10 sundried tomatoes (dry-packed)
6 to 8 sage leaves
Pinch each nutmeg and cayenne
½ cup (125 mL) grated asiago
1¼ cups (300 mL) fusilli or rotini
Sea salt and fresh pepper
Parmesan, optional

Peach Crumble

1½ lb (750 g) peaches (about 6)
2 tbsp (25 mL) lemon juice
3 tbsp (45 mL) granulated sugar
½ cup (125 mL) plus 1 tsp (5 mL) all-purpose flour
Large pinch ground ginger
3 tbsp (45 mL) butter
½ cup (125 mL) rolled oats
¼ cup (50 mL) brown sugar
Large pinch nutmeg

MENU FOR TWO

Fried Green Tomato Salad

Roasted Vegetable Pie

Citrus-Scented Couscous

Spiced Spelt Cake

Toward the end of September, my tomato plants, unaware of the cruel fate the coming frost holds for them, continue to flower and produce fruit. These green tomatoes, which are often small, are plentiful in my kitchen at this time. Great for salsas and relishes, the pleasingly tart fruits are also terrific tossed in cornmeal, quickly sautéed and served over greens. Fans of Fannie Flagg's great book *Fried Green Tomatoes at the Whistle Stop Café* could glance back over its pages for her recipe for southern-style thick slabs of green tomato.

FOOD FOR ART'S SAKE

The core of this meal is a crisp roasted vegetable pie with a citrus-scented couscous.

I thrill to see my love of food (some call it an obsession) paralleled in popular culture. Peter Mayle's *A Year in Provence* had me hooked from the first sentence: "The year began with lunch." I knew this was a book to appeal to the literary gastronome in me. And of course, I couldn't put down *Like Water for Chocolate* or Canadian writer Gail Anderson-Dargatz's award-winning *The Cure for Death by Lightening* or John Lanchester's ghoulishly funny *The Debt to Pleasure*. Then there are the movies! To sit in the dark and watch the beauty and passion of food displayed in visual poetry on the big screen is sheer joy. *Babette's Feast, Big Night* and *Eat, Drink, Man, Woman* are just three of the films I could watch over and over again. I am not a fan of brutality in any form, so it is difficult for me to watch *The Cook, The Thief, His Wife and Her Lover* for the many disturbing scenes it contains, but I have sat through it half a dozen times for the stunning kitchen imagery. These moments of pure pleasure are the cherry on the cake of my day.

The core of this meal is a crisp, roasted vegetable pie with citrus-scented couscous. My favourite thing about this pie is the way the vegetables come out cooked but still quite crunchy. If you would like a sauce to serve with it, nothing could be more simple than whisking 1 tbsp (15 mL) grainy Dijon mustard into ¼ cup (50 mL) of whipping cream and letting it reduce over medium heat until it coats the back of a spoon.

Spelt flour is made from an ancient cereal grain suitable for people on wheat-free diets. Many people avoid wheat due to difficulties digesting the grain, and finding foods and recipes to accommodate such a diet can be a challenge. Spelt and kamut are the two flours I use most for wheat-free baking because they have excellent nutritional value and are still high in gluten. Gluten is the protein in wheat that helps in the leavening process so these ancient grains can produce a light cake or bread, whereas gluten-free flours, like those made of rice or beans, tend to result in a heavy, hard product. My heart goes out to those unfortunate souls with celiac disease as they must avoid all gluten and the soft luxury of biting into a well-made bread is forever lost for them. However, even for those who tolerate wheat well, it is a good dietary practice to vary the foods we eat, including the flours we use to bake.

0:00 Make a brief stop at the video store to rent something delicious to watch after dinner. Once home again, preheat the oven to 350°F (180°C).

0:01 *To prepare the vegetable pie:* Butter a 4-cup (1-L) glass baking dish and dust it with flour. Slice the zucchini lengthwise and use the strips to line the bottom and sides of the dish. Lightly season the zucchini with salt and pepper. Peel and grate the carrot, parsnip and squash. Mix together the eggs, cream, salt, nutmeg, cayenne and minced garlic. Toss the grated vegetables in the egg mixture, pour it into the zucchini-lined dish and bake it, covered, for 45 minutes.

0:20 *For the spelt cake:* If necessary, place the butter in the oven for a moment to melt. In a medium-sized bowl, mix together the flour, sugar, nuts, baking powder, baking soda, ginger, nutmeg, allspice and cinnamon. Make a well in the flour mixture and add the egg, milk and butter. Stir until they are just mixed (don't worry about a few lumps) and pour the batter into a buttered 7-inch (17.5-cm) cake pan. Bake the cake on the middle rack of the oven for 20 minutes or until the cake springs back to the touch and a toothpick inserted in the centre comes out clean. When you are ready to serve the cake, dust it with icing sugar and cocoa.

CATHERINE'S WINE TIP

Yikes! What a menu. It's tough to compete with such a variety of flavours. However, a good young Italian Chianti will go a long way toward mustering up the balance this meal wants.

0:35 *To make couscous:* Remove the zest from the orange and lemon halves. Juice the orange and lemon and add enough water to make ½ cup (125 mL) liquid. Place the liquid in a small pan on the stove. Add salt until it tastes a little salty. Bring the liquid to a boil and add the oil. Stir in the couscous until the liquid is absorbed. Transfer the couscous to a small bowl and cover it tightly with plastic wrap. After 5 minutes, fluff it with a fork and replace the wrap. Fluff the couscous again just before serving so each piece is separate. To serve the couscous hot, prepare all the ingredients but wait to stir the couscous into the boiling liquid until after the main course. Let it sit for 5 minutes, fluff and serve.

0:50 *For the salad:* Place the greens on two salad plates and sprinkle them with salt and pepper. If the tomatoes are large, cut them into 1-inch (2.5-cm) cubes. Smaller tomatoes can be quartered. Stir ½ tsp (2 mL) salt into the cornmeal. Dredge the tomatoes in flour, then egg, then cornmeal. Heat the oil in a pan over high heat, then quickly sauté the tomatoes until they are browned. Toss in the basil. Spoon warm tomatoes and basil over the greens and drizzle them with balsamic vinegar. Serve immediately.

Fried Green Tomato Salad

2 handfuls baby greens
½ tsp (2 mL) sea salt plus sea salt to taste
Fresh pepper
8 oz (250 g) green tomatoes
2 tbsp (25 mL) flour
1 egg, beaten
2 tbsp (25 mL) cornmeal
½ cup (125 mL) olive oil
2 tbsp (25 mL) chopped basil
2 tbsp (25 mL) balsamic vinegar

Roasted Vegetable Pie

2 tbsp (25 mL) flour
1 zucchini
Sea salt and fresh pepper
1 carrot
1 parsnip
5 oz (150 g) squash
2 eggs
¼ cup (50 mL) whipping cream
¼ tsp (50 mL) salt
Pinch nutmeg
Pinch cayenne
1 clove minced garlic

Citrus-Scented Couscous

½ orange
½ lemon
Sea salt
1 tbsp (15 mL) oil
½ cup (125 mL) couscous

Spiced Spelt Cake

2 tbsp (25 mL) butter, melted
1 cup (250 mL) spelt flour
¼ cup (50 mL) sugar
½ cup (125 mL) ground nuts
1 tsp (5 mL) baking powder
¼ tsp (1 mL) baking soda
¼ tsp (1 mL) ginger

MENU FOR TWO

Potato and Garlic Soup

Wild Mushroom Bread Pudding

Roasted Quails

Apple Crisp

September is such a sentimental month. Darker days, colder nights and the bitter-sweet ending to a long, hot summer are tempered by the comfort of harvest. Kurt Weill captured the mood perfectly in his "September Song," with its haunting melancholy and sense of yearning for things past. A roaring fire, some cognac and a collection of Weill music set the mood for sipping and reminiscing on a cold, rainy, autumn night.

REMEMBERING PROVENCE

A roaring fire, some cognac, and Weill's September Song sets the mood for reminiscing.

And to fuel this brooding mood, how about a soothing fall feast? Bread pudding is a favourite of mine because it's fast, foolproof and simply soul warming. Challah (egg bread) works best, mixed with eggs and cream and whatever other flavours you wish. The wild mushrooms featured in this menu make a fantastic savoury pudding redolent of fresh herbs and garlic. Choose portobello, oyster or any fresh, wild mushrooms. Other versions of this pudding can be prepared with caramelized onions or fresh sage and strong cheese. Apples and cinnamon or pear and almond added to the same basic ingredients will produce a lovely dessert.

The potato and garlic soup, like many of my favourite dishes, had its origins in the kitchen of Elie Benchitrit. Elie is the owner of Provence restaurant in Toronto and I had the pleasure of working in his kitchen. Elie is the type of restaurant owner who has a very hands-on approach, working closely with the chef. I was always pleased because I knew that when Elie came into the kitchen, I was certain to learn something new about Provençal cooking. Elie's soup was different from mine, omitting the cream and favouring water over chicken stock, but nonetheless I owe its uncomplicated good taste to him.

Quail are wonderful, slightly gamy little birds, perfectly suited to quick roasting because of their size. They can be served whole and stuffed, as in this menu, or, when time permits, with the backbone and ribcage removed. However, the boning can be time consuming if you are not accustomed to working with such a small bird. To accomplish the task, slide a sharp knife from the neck opening to the bottom of the spine and cut through on each side of the backbone to remove it, along with the neck. Then use a small boning knife to cut away the rig cage and breastbone. The boned quail can be quickly pan-fried or grilled and served with polenta and a sauce made from the bones. To make the sauce, brown the bones along with some sliced onions in a small pan and then deglaze the pan with a splash of calvados or brandy and cover it all with chicken stock. Let the mixture simmer for 10 minutes, then strain it. Place the jus back in the pan, reduce by half, then garnish with some fresh berries and finish with cold butter by quickly stirring it into the sauce.

September is also the month for apples and I have included them in the recipes for both the quails and the dessert. Cubes of sweet apple make a quick stuffing to support our birds while they're cooking and the apple is delicious after roasting. Apple crisp was my mother's specialty. Her version was made with very little butter in the topping and deemed a suitable low-fat dessert when she was dieting. As she rarely weighed more than a hundred pounds, my diminutive mother was always dieting, so even the low-fat version was a welcome treat. Still, mom's recipe aside, I like a more buttery topping because it crisps up so well, and after all, it is apple crisp.

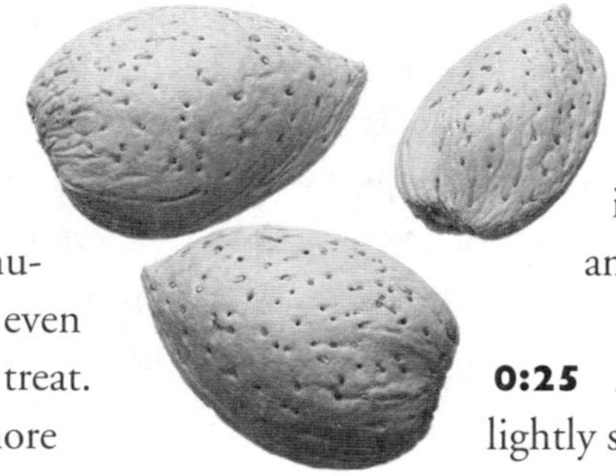

0:00 Turn down the 20th-century Germanic pop opera; you're depressing me. Open instead a bottle of Spanish Rioja and let some light-heartedness into the kitchen. Chill a bottle of Canadian Late Harvest Riesling to have with dessert.

0:01 Preheat oven to 400°C (200°C).
For the soup: Peel the potatoes and cut them into 1-inch (2.5-cm) cubes. Mince the garlic and slice the onions. Brown the potatoes and onions in oil over a medium high heat. Stir to prevent sticking. Add the garlic. Deglaze the pot with lemon juice by scraping any bits from the bottom with a wooden spoon. Add the stock, bring to a boil and reduce to simmer. Cook, covered, until the potatoes are very tender, about 30 minutes.

0:10 While the soup is simmering, prepare the bread pudding: Butter two 1¼ cup (350 mL) baking dishes. Sauté the mushrooms in 2 tbsp (25 mL) butter until they are soft. Deglaze the pan with the brandy, then remove it from heat. Add the milk and stir in the eggs. Season with salt and pepper. Trim the slices of challah to fit the baking dishes and place one piece in the bottom of each dish. Pour half the mushroom mix over the bread and fit the second piece of challah on top. Pour the remaining mushroom mix over the bread and set the dishes aside.

0:25 *For the quails:* Wash the quails and lightly salt and pepper them inside and out.

Cube the apple and stuff the cubes into each bird's cavity. Rub the mustard on the breasts and legs and cover them with the almonds. Place the birds in a shallow baking pan and bake them for 30 minutes or until a knife inserted at the thigh joint causes the juices to run clear.

0:40 *To finish the soup:* Purée the soup in a food processor and stir in cream. If necessary, adjust the consistency: if it's too thin, return it to the heat to reduce; if it's too thick, stir in some extra stock or water and return to it to the stove to bring the temperature up. Keep the soup warm over a low heat until you're ready to serve it. Place the bread pudding in the oven to bake for 15 minutes or until the eggs have set and the top is browned.

0:45 *For apple crisp:* Mix together the dry ingredients. Rub in cold, cubed butter until the texture is coarse and pebbly. Peel the apples and cut them into 1-inch (2.5-cm) slices. Divide the apples into two buttered 1½-cup (250-mL) baking dishes. Cover both with the topping. When the quail and the bread pudding are removed from the oven, reduce the heat to 350°F (180°C) and bake the apple crisp for 50 minutes.

Potato and Garlic Soup

2 medium potatoes
5 cloves garlic
1 small onion
1 tbsp (15 mL) olive oil
2 tbsp (25 mL) lemon juice
2 cups (500 mL) chicken stock
¼ cup (50 mL) whipping cream

Wild Mushroom Bread Pudding

2 cups (500 mL) sliced wild mushrooms
2 tbsp (25 mL) butter
2 tbsp (25 mL) brandy
¾ cup (175 mL) milk
2 eggs, beaten
¼ tsp (1 mL) each sea salt and fresh pepper
4 ¾-inch (2-cm) slices challah (egg bread)

Roasted Quails

4 quails
Sea salt and fresh pepper
1 apple
2 tsp (10 mL) Dijon mustard
2 tbsp (25 mL) almonds

Apple Crisp

3 tbsp (45 mL) sugar
3 tbsp (45 mL) oats
3 tbsp (45 mL) flour
Pinch salt
Pinch nutmeg
Pinch ginger
¼ tsp (1 mL) cinnamon
3 tbsp (45 mL) cold butter
4 medium, tart baking apples

MENU FOR FOUR

Antipasto

Cornish Hens in Roasted Shallot and Portobello Mushroom Sauce

Spinach Risotto

Pomegranates and Caramelized Lemon

It seems I keep coming back to Italy. When asked if I have a favourite national cuisine, I always refrain from choosing. I have found fantastic food everywhere I have travelled and part of the great fortune of being Canadian is easy access to people, cultures and food from around the globe. Working in the restaurant kitchens of Toronto, I have known wonderful cooks from France, Italy, Spain, Sri Lanka, China and dozens of other countries. Put two cooks in a room with a stovetop and I guarantee you they will talk about little else but food; talk will lead to action and soon enough they will be trading secrets. I will be forever grateful for all the wonderful knowledge passed on to me by the eclectic mix of talented cooks and chefs I have known. And still, I keep coming back to Italy.

PERSEPHONE'S POMEGRANATES AND MORE FROM CULINARY HEAVEN

Persephone, unable to resist three pomegranate seeds, was banished to Hades each year.

What most appeals to me about Italian cuisine is its purity. Flavours are simple, yet astonishing in their vibrancy. The tomato. Basil. Olives. A cookbook could be written in tribute to each of these ingredients.

Fresh vegetables, herbs and grains are at the centre of Italian cooking and are brilliantly married to regional cheeses, meats and seafood. Magnificent breads, fresh pastas, rice and ancient grains are celebrated in this truly healthful, absolutely splendid approach to food. It is no wonder that Italian cuisine has caught the imagination of the world. And I haven't even mentioned the temptations of the bakery! Or the wine. From Alto Adige to Sicily, the nectar of the gods, the bounty of the grape, is abundant throughout this culinary heaven.

Many home cooks I have met are intimidated by the idea of making risotto. Follow a few basic rules and the result should be rich, creamy and perfect every time. Toast the arborio rice first in oil or butter, then add the hot stock slowly so it just covers the rice. Stir, stir, stir and continue to add more stock only after the rice has absorbed the previous liquid. The finished dish should be creamy, with each individual kernel of rice still firm to the bite.

I cannot eat pomegranates without thinking of Persephone. She was the daughter of Demeter, the Greek goddess of agriculture, responsible for the fruitfulness of the earth and humankind. Pluto (aka Hades) abducted or seduced—depending on whom you talk to—innocent young Persephone and carried her off to his kingdom in the underworld (aka Hell). In her grief and fury, Demeter froze the earth and threatened to destroy all humanity by withdrawing her bounty. Zeus interceded, but sadly Persephone had violated a law forbidding her to eat or drink while she was in the underworld. She had been unable to resist the charms of three tiny pomegranate seeds and so was doomed to spend six months of every year at Hades' side. Demeter responded by changing the earth to a barren, cold land until Persephone's return in the spring.

Obviously, an Italian wine is a must for this menu, and a medium-bodied red would be my choice; a Barolo or Barbaresco would do nicely.

0:00 Preheat the oven to 400°F (200°C). If your long day has resembled Persephone's months with Hades, take a moment to enjoy the warmth and comfort of your kitchen. If you hate your kitchen as much as your job, feel comforted by the knowledge that in one short hour you will be treating yourself to a meal fit for the gods.

0:01 *For the pomegranate:* Split the pomegranate in half and scoop out the seeds with a spoon or your fingers. I find using my fingers works best. Pour lemon juice and Grand Marnier over top, cover and refrigerate. Remove the zest from the lemon. A zester makes this easy but if you don't have one, cut away the peel in strips. Use a small, sharp knife to remove any bitter, white pith adhering to the peel and then julienne it.

0:10 *To prepare the hens:* Wash the hens and sprinkle salt and pepper over both the outside and inside. Stuff each one with unpeeled garlic cloves, place them in a roasting pan and rub the top sides with butter. Peel all the shallots, reserve 2 oz (50 g) for the risotto and place the remainder, whole, in the roasting pan. Wash the mushrooms, pat them dry and break off the stems. Cut the stems into ½-inch (1-cm) slices and place them in roasting pan. Drizzle 1 tbsp (15 mL) olive oil over the shallots and mushrooms stems and place the roasting pan in the oven for 45 minutes. Cut the mushroom tops into ¼-inch (6-mm) slices and sauté them in 2 tbsp (25 mL) olive oil until they are soft. Set them aside.

0:30 *Begin the risotto:* Chop the shallots and cook them in 2 tbsp (25 mL) butter over a high heat until they are soft. Stir in the rice and cook it until it is lightly toasted. Add ¾ cup (175 mL) stock and stir until the liquid is absorbed. Keep adding stock and stirring until you have ½ cup (125 mL) left. Check the spinach for grittiness and, if necessary, wash and pick out any large stems; then chop it up. Add the spinach to the risotto with the last of the stock and stir it until the spinach is wilted. If you are using store-bought stock, the risotto will likely not require salting, so be sure to taste before seasoning. Stir in 2 tsp (10 mL) butter. Serve with shaved parmesan over top.

0:45 *Assemble the antipasto:* Remember to give the risotto a stir every few minutes while putting this together. Place the kale or lettuce along one side of a large platter. Layer the prosciutto and provolone on the bottom and finish with the artichokes, olives and peppers. Drizzle olive oil over the lot and sprinkle with freshly ground pepper. Place the platter in the centre of the table and allow guests to help themselves. Offer some nice Calabrese bread to go with it.

0:60 The hens should be ready to come out of the oven by the time the appetizers are finished.

To make the sauce: Remove the hens from the roasting pan and discard the garlic, which was intended to impart flavour and brace the bird as it cooks. (Unless you are a fan of raw garlic, it is not quite roasted enough to eat.) Deglaze the pan with red wine by scraping the bits from the bottom of the pan with a wooden spoon, over a medium high heat. Add the stock and bring the mixture to a boil. Remove the mushroom stems and pour the shallots and jus over the cooked portobello tops. Place the portobello pan over the heat and stir in the tomato paste. Serve each guest half a hen with the sauce over top and the risotto on the side.

When you are ready to serve the ice cream: Place the sugar and 2 tbsp (25 mL) cold water in a small saucepan over a high heat. When the sugar has dissolved and the solution begins to thicken, about 2 to 3 minutes, add the zest. Let the mixture cook until the sugar begins to caramelize, about 3 more minutes, and remove from heat. As always, when working with caramel, exercise extreme caution as it is unbelievably hot. Resist every temptation to stick your fingers in it—you will be badly burned. Scoop the ice cream into four dessert bowls and cover each with the pomegranate and liqueur. While the caramelized lemon zest is still hot, spoon it over top—it will harden in seconds for a stunning presentation.

Antipasto

4 to 6 leaves purple kale or red leaf lettuce
3 oz (90 g) prosciutto, thinly sliced
3 oz (90 g) provolone cheese, sliced
8 pieces artichoke hearts
¼ cup (50 mL) marinated black olives
¼ cup (50 mL) roasted, marinated red peppers
2 tbsp (25 mL) olive oil
Calabrese bread

Cornish Hens in Roasted Shallot and Portobello Mushroom Sauce

2 Cornish hens
Sea salt and fresh pepper
8 cloves garlic
1 tbsp (15 mL) butter
6 oz (170 g) shallots
1 lb (500 g) portobello mushrooms
3 tbsp (45 mL) olive oil
⅓ cup (75 mL) red wine
⅓ cup (75 mL) chicken stock
2 tsp (5 mL) tomato paste

Spinach Risotto

2 oz (50 g) shallots
2 tbsp plus 2 tsp (55 mL) butter
½ cup (125 mL) arborio rice
3 cups (750 mL) chicken stock
10 oz (300 g) prewashed spinach
2 oz (50 g) parmesan

Pomegranates and Caramelized Lemon

1 pomegranate
2 tbsp (25 mL) lemon juice
3 tbsp (45 mL) Grand Marnier
1 lemon
2 tbsp (25 mL) sugar
2 tbsp (25 mL) cold water
1 cup (250 mL) vanilla ice cream
2 tbsp (25 mL) brown sugar
⅓ cup (75 mL) ground hazelnuts

MENU FOR TWO

Savoury Corn Pudding

Bouillabaisse

Autumn Cobbler

Once, on the shores of the Mediterranean, hungry Provençal fishermen would build a fire under a cauldron that held some of the day's catch and a few fresh herbs. In minutes they could warm themselves with a bowl of steaming hot bouillabaisse. The name comes from the French words *bouillir* (to boil) and *abaisser* (to reduce). This flavourful stew has been adopted and adapted by cooks the world over—today there are probably as many recipes for bouillabaisse as there are fish in the sea. About 20 years ago, the restaurateurs of Marseilles, France, attempted to write the official bouillabaisse charter to record the "authentic" recipe, but even in the dish's ancestral home, no one has been able to agree on one true version. There is, however, a single point on which everyone agrees: The fish must be fresh. At the fish counter, use your sense of smell. Fresh fish is practically odourless, so if you detect a whiff of something unpleasant or anything remotely resembling ammonia, do not buy it. Sunken or cloudy eyes mean the fish has been days out of the sea. Gills should be red, the skin dry (not slimy) and the scales firmly attached. When buying a fillet or steak already cut from the whole fish, check that the flesh is translucent, not cloudy, and, in the case of steaks, that the flesh is not falling off the bone.

AUTUMN SOOTHER

Even in Marseilles, no one can agree what is "authentic" bouillabaisse.

Shellfish is another matter. Clams, mussels and oysters should be alive and their shells should be tightly closed when you buy them. Scrub the shells under cold running water to remove any grit (cold water will cause clams to close more tightly). Any that remain open after cleaning should be discarded, as should any with cracked shells. Once cooked, the shells will open fully; throw away any that remain stubbornly closed. With shellfish, it is always best to err on the side of caution.

Rockfish is central to the bouillabaisses of Marseilles, but I have substituted readily available sea bass and monkfish. For shellfish, I have chosen cherrystone clams, snow crab claws and jumbo shrimp, but you can substitute any of your favourites. Smaller clams such as littlenecks, king crab legs and lobster tails are just a few options. A more affordable version might feature cultured mussels, smaller shrimp and fish. There are only a few guidelines: Try to use fresh or fresh-frozen fish and shellfish, include a mixture of fin fish and shellfish, and avoid fatty or oily fish such as salmon or mackerel.

Toasted slices of baguette slathered with rouille, a red pepper mayonnaise, often accompany bouillabaisse. If you have the time before starting the meal, you can make this simple MOCK ROUILLE: Combine 3 tbsp (45 mL) mayonnaise with ½ tsp (2 mL) minced garlic, ¼ tsp (1 mL) lemon juice, and a pinch each of paprika, saffron, cayenne and salt. Just before serving, whisk in 1 tsp (5 mL) bouillabaisse broth.

November is the perfect month for the nurturing cook. Icy rains and cold winds bring my family indoors to be warmed and fed from the pantry I have been stocking for months. I naturally begin to cook comfort foods such as Savoury Corn Pudding and Autumn Cobbler. Both the appetizer and dessert are served hot from the oven; each possesses a sturdiness of texture and flavour designed to soothe and sate a late-autumn hunger.

0:00 Pour yourself a glass of Vin de Cassis or Côtes de Provence Rosé and imagine yourself in Provence.

0:01 Preheat oven to 350°F (180°C). Make a bain marie by filling an 8-inch (2-L) square baking dish halfway up the sides with hot water and placing it in the middle rack of the oven. Grease two 1¼-cup (300 mL) custard pots with a little butter, then dust them with a little cornmeal. Dice the red pepper and finely slice the green onions. Place them in a mixing bowl. Add 1 tsp (5 mL) thyme leaves. Scald the milk until it is just steaming (do not let it boil). Whisk 2 tbsp (25 mL) cornmeal into the milk until the mixture has thickened slightly, about 1 minute. Remove it from the heat. Whisk the eggs, ¼ tsp (1 mL) salt, pepper to taste and cayenne into the red pepper and onion mixture. Crumble in chèvre. Whisk in the hot milk and cornmeal. Add corn kernels, pour into prepared custard pots and place them in the bain marie in the oven. The puddings will be ready in 30 minutes or when set in the middle.

0:15 Peel and core apples; cut each into six wedges. Combine with blackberries and brown sugar. Toss them well to coat the fruit with sugar. (This prevents the fruit from losing its colour.) Put the fruit into a buttered 4-cup (1-L) baking dish. Mix together the hazelnuts, flour, granulated sugar, baking powder and salt. Cut the butter into small cubes and rub it into the flour using your fingers until the texture is coarse and mealy. The more you mix now, the less you will need to do after adding the liquid, when overworking is more of a concern. Stir in 3 tbsp (45 mL) milk until the dough just forms.

0:30 Press the dough over the fruit; place the pan in oven. Bake it 40 to 45 minutes.
Prepare the leek: Trim away the dark green top, roots and coarse outer layer. Cut it in half lengthwise and wash it well under cold water, separating each layer to remove trapped dirt. Chop the leek and garlic.

0:35 Rinse the seafood under cold water. Scrub crab and clam shells well; discard cracked shells and any clams that do not close tightly. Cut the monkfish and sea bass in half.

0:40 Heat the oil in a large heavy-bottomed pot over a medium heat. Stir in the leek, garlic, fennel, saffron, orange zest and thyme sprigs. Add the clams; cook the mixture, uncovered, 5 minutes.

0:45 Check the puddings. If they are set in the middle, remove them from oven and keep them warm in the bain marie. Add the monkfish, sea bass, crab and shrimp to the bouillabaisse and stir. Add the tomatoes, bay leaf, stock and ¼ tsp (1 mL) salt. Raise heat to medium high and bring the soup to a boil. Lower the heat; let the soup simmer 10 minutes, uncovered. When fully cooked, the shrimp and crab should be bright pink, the fish should be white through to the middle and the clams should be fully opened. Discard any clams that do not open, along with bay leaf and thyme.

0:55 Serve the puddings in their cups or inverted on a plate garnished with fresh thyme sprigs. To serve the broth and seafood separately, remove the seafood with a slotted spoon and arrange in two shallow bowls. Garnish them with fennel fronds. If you are not serving rouille, line the bottom of a small tureen with thick slices of baguette and pour the broth over top. If you are serving rouille, fill the tureen with broth first, then garnish with toasted slices of baguette and a dollop of the mayonnaise.

1:10 Test the cobbler for doneness by pushing a toothpick into the topping—it should come out clean. The apples should be tender. Remove the cobbler from the oven and let it rest while you finish your meal. This cobbler yields four servings; save the leftovers for another night.

Savoury Corn Pudding

¼ cup (50 mL) each red pepper and green onions
1 tsp (5 mL) fresh thyme or ½ tsp (2 mL) dried thyme
1 cup (250 mL) whole milk
2 tbsp (25 mL) cornmeal
2 large eggs
¼ tsp (1 mL) sea salt
Pepper
Pinch cayenne
2 oz (60 g) chèvre
½ cup (125 mL) raw corn kernels

Bouillabaisse

1 leek
3 cloves garlic
7 oz (210 g) snow crab claws
4 cherrystone clams
6 oz (170 g) each monkfish fillet and sea bass fillet
4 jumbo shrimp, peeled and cleaned
2 tbsp (25 mL) olive oil
¼ cup (50 mL) chopped fennel bulb, fronds reserved for garnish, or ¼ tsp (1 mL) fennel seeds
Pinch saffron
1 tsp (5 mL) orange zest
5 sprigs fresh thyme
4 canned plum tomatoes
1 bay leaf
1 cup (250 mL) fish stock or water
¼ tsp (1 mL) sea salt
1 baguette
Mock rouille, optional

Autumn Cobbler

2 Granny Smith apples
1 cup (250 mL) blackberries or blueberries
2 tbsp (25 mL) brown sugar
⅓ cup (75 mL) each ground hazelnuts and all-purpose flour
2 tbsp (25 mL) granulated sugar
2 tsp (10 mL) baking powder
Pinch salt
2 tbsp (25 mL) unsalted butter, cold
3 tbsp (45 mL) milk

MENU FOR TWO

Watercress and Garlic Soup

Mint-Crusted Tenderloin

Mashed Sweet Potato

Apricot Cake

In my family, our love was often shown through the foods we shared. My grandmother baked me peanut butter cookies and chocolate chip cookies. And although she never made me eat my vegetables, she did have a knack for making them palatable. My mother cooked savoury foods that comforted me through the thousand shocks that are part of growing up.

FROM THE HEART

> *My mother cooked me foods that comforted me through a thousand shocks.*

My mother and grandmothers inspired me to write *Recipes for Homemade Love*, a cookbook and oral history of a century of Canadian home cooking. I spoke to friends, strangers and famous cooks across Canada, recording stories, family folklore and recipes passed down from earlier generations.

This month's menu is a tribute to a few of my own family traditions. The watercress soup is inspired by the hearty broths and purées my mother cooked to keep autumn's chill at bay. It is also evidence of my mother's resourcefulness with ducks. She would buy four ducks, make confit with the legs and extra fat, panfry the breasts and use the carcasses to make a rich broth, ideal for tempering watercress's bitter charm. If you have neither the time nor the inclination to trifle with duck, chicken stock can be substituted.

The crisp, minty, crusted pork loin is a smaller version of a dish I remember from my grandmother's groaning board. She was always more interested in the social joys of cooking, so most of her recipes were simple, adding flavour in seconds, using tricks such as tossing a few whole onions and apples into the roasting pan. Mashed sweet potato was one of her clever ploys to encourage vegetable consumption among the younger family members—and it worked. The pickiest eaters could not resist something so smooth, sweet and creamy.

Save the wine for the main course and choose a light Beaujolais or a big, fruity white such as a Pinot Gris.

0:00 Take a minute to think about your great-grandmother's kitchen, then thank the kitchen gods for indoor plumbing, modern appliances and stores that sell more types of food than she could ever have imagined.

0:01 *Roast garlic for soup:* Heat the oven to 450°F (230°C). Cut off the top of the garlic bulb to expose the tips of cloves. Place the bulb on a baking sheet; drizzle ¼ tsp (1 mL) olive oil over it. Sprinkle sugar over top and salt and pepper it to taste. Roast the garlic until it is golden and soft, 25 minutes.

0:05 *For apricot cake:* Grease a 5- by 2½-inch (15- by 6-cm) mini loaf pan. Cream together the butter and sugar, then beat in the egg. Stir in the apricot nectar. (The mixture will curdle.) In another bowl, sift together the flour, ginger, baking powder and salt. Mix the dry ingredients into the wet. Pour the batter into the prepared loaf pan and set it aside.

0:15 *For tenderloin:* In a food processor, chop the granola and mint until mixture is the consistency of coarse crumbs. Mix the crumbs with applesauce and mustard. Place the pork on a foil-lined baking sheet; lightly season it with salt and pepper. Brush it with beaten egg; use a spatula to cover the exposed sides with the granola mixture. Set it aside.

0:25 Remove the garlic from the oven and set it aside. Turn the oven to 350°F (180°C). Place the cake in oven; bake it for 35 to 40 minutes or until a toothpick comes out clean.
For mashed sweet potato: Peel the potato and cut it into 2-inch (5-cm) cubes. Place the cubes in a medium saucepan and cover with a generous amount of cold salted water. Bring it to a boil over high heat. Meanwhile, peel the sweet potato and cut it into 1-inch (2.5-cm) cubes. When the water boils, add the sweet potato. Cook the potatoes, uncovered, until they are fork tender, about 20 minutes.

0:35 *For the soup:* Chop the shallot. Remove the tough larger stems from the watercress. Squeeze the roasted garlic from its skin. In a medium saucepan, heat 2 tsp (10 mL) olive oil over medium, then add butter. Sauté the shallot, watercress and roasted garlic until the greens have wilted. Add the stock; bring the mixture to a boil. Reduce the heat and simmer it for 5 minutes. Purée the soup, then return it to low heat and stir in the cream. Let it cook 1 minute, then add the vinegar and salt and pepper to taste. Keep the soup warm until you are ready to serve it.

0:50 Cut the onion into quarters. Cut the apple in half. Place the onion and apple cut sides up next to the tenderloin. Drizzle olive oil over the apple and onion. Season them with sugar and a pinch each salt and pepper. Place the pork in the oven next to the cake. Roast it for 20 minutes.

0:55 Remove the cake from the oven. Drain the potatoes, then return them to a low heat for 2 minutes to dry. Using a hand masher, mash the potatoes with milk and butter, then season with nutmeg, cayenne and salt and pepper to taste. Keep the potatoes warm until ready to serve.

0:60 Serve the soup. When pork has roasted 20 minutes, move it to the top oven rack. Turn off the oven, then set it to broil. Broil the pork for 2 minutes or until the crust is golden and crisp and the meat has just a hint of pink at its centre. Separate the onion layers into petals and divide them between two plates. Slice the tenderloin diagonally and arrange the slices on the onion petals. Top them with the apple and serve with mashed sweet potato.

For dessert, dust slices of cake with icing sugar; serve with apricots if available.

Watercress and Garlic Soup

1 bulb garlic
¼ tsp (1 mL) plus 2 tsp (10 mL) olive oil
Pinch granulated sugar
Sea salt and fresh pepper
1 shallot
1 bunch watercress
1 tbsp (15 mL) butter
2 cups (500 mL) duck or chicken stock
2 tbsp (25 mL) whipping cream
1 tsp (5 mL) balsamic vinegar

Mint-Crusted Tenderloin

¼ cup (50 mL) fruit and nut granola
10 mint leaves
1 tbsp (15 mL) each applesauce and Dijon mustard
10 oz (300 g) pork tenderloin
Sea salt and fresh pepper
1 egg, lightly beaten
1 onion
1 apple
1 tsp (5 mL) olive oil
¼ tsp (1 mL) granulated sugar

Mashed Sweet Potato

1 medium Yukon Gold potato
1 small sweet potato
3 tbsp (45 mL) milk
1 tbsp (15 mL) butter
Pinch each nutmeg and cayenne
Sea salt and fresh pepper

Apricot Cake

⅓ cup (75 mL) each butter, softened and granulated sugar
1 egg, at room temperature
⅓ cup (75 mL) apricot nectar, at room temperature
½ cup (125 mL) all-purpose flour
½ tsp (2 mL) ground ginger
¼ tsp (1 mL) baking powder
Pinch salt
1 tbsp (15 mL) icing sugar
2 apricots or plums, optional

MENU FOR FOUR

Squash and Apple Soup
with Crème Fraîche

Maple-Glazed Ham with
Autumn Fruits and Vegetables

Pumpkin Pie with
White Chocolate Liqueur

Thanksgiving at my house as I was growing up meant listening to my mother get up at dawn to start the bird. She would spend the better part of the day preparing the turkey and concocting a host of side dishes, from fresh cranberry sauce to persimmon chutney. Once served, the meal would vanish in minutes. My mother would be too exhausted to enjoy the meal herself and usually ended up prostrate in bed soon after dinner, where her children served her dessert. While Thanksgiving is a marvellous time to celebrate the harvest bounty by preparing an elaborate feast, it can be refreshing to serve an easy dinner that leaves the cook enough energy to enjoy the social side of the day.

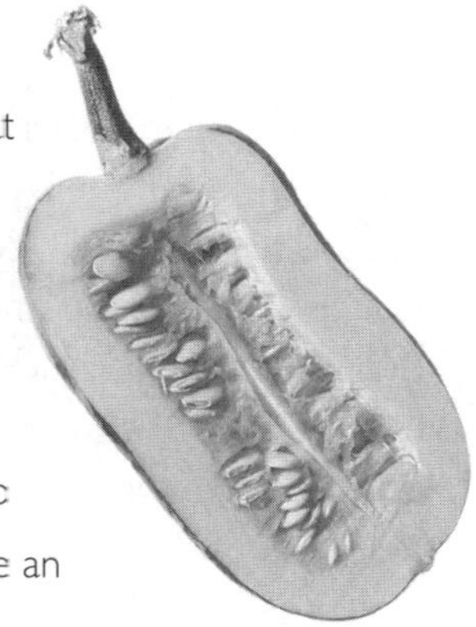

HAM FOR THE HOLIDAYS

This Thanksgiving dinner will leave you, in 1 hour, with nothing to do but enjoy the praise.

Help is at hand. For this month's menu, I have devised a festive dinner that won't have you chained to the stove for hours on end. All the elements of a classic Thanksgiving dinner are on the menu. Apple gives a butternut squash soup a full harvest flavour. Sour cream can easily replace crème fraîche as a garnish. If you have a spare moment the night before, try preparing your own CRÈME FRAÎCHE: Combine 1 cup (250 mL) whipping cream with 1 tbsp (15 mL) buttermilk. (This recipe can easily be halved.) Let sit, covered, in a warm spot, overnight or for 12 hours. Then refrigerate until dinnertime. Leftover crème fraîche will keep, refrigerated, for 2 to 3 weeks and can be used to finish a sauce without fear of curdling it.

Serving a ham is traditional in many homes and is infinitely more simple than roasting a turkey because there is no need for stuffing, trussing or basting. Its smaller size also makes it a better choice for an intimate gathering. In this maple-sweet version, cranberries and figs are roasted with whole chestnuts, garlic cloves, vegetables and sage in a single dish that will satisfy both the adventurous palate and the most exacting traditionalist. Fresh chestnuts usually appear in stores in October. If they don't arrive by Thanksgiving, substitute the canned variety or shelled hazelnuts.

Whether your pastry is store-bought or homemade, pumpkin pie is sure to please. Here, the filling is laced with white chocolate cream liqueur (available in 4-oz/50 mL bottles). A frozen crust for the pumpkin pie is the best choice for the cook in a hurry. If you do have the time to make your own, try this recipe for SPICED PIE PASTRY. In a food processor, combine 1½ cups (375 mL) all-purpose flour, 3 tbsp (45 mL) granulated sugar, ½ tsp (2 mL) ground cinnamon and ¼ tsp (1 mL) each ground ginger, nutmeg and sea salt. Cube ¾ cup (175 mL) cold butter and pulse into flour until it has the texture of coarse meal; don't worry about overworking the dough at this stage. In fact, it is better to work it well now so you can handle it less after you add the water. Empty the dough into a bowl and add 2 tbsp (25 mL) ice water, 1 tbsp (15 mL) at a time, until the dough holds together when pressed into a ball; less handling at this stage will give you a more tender end product. Wrap the dough in plastic and refrigerate for at least 1 hour. Roll out the dough and transfer to a 9-inch (23-cm) pie plate. Refrigerate, covered, until baking time.

To complement your meal, I recommend a Gewürztraminer. The sweetness of maple syrup and fruit will cause many drier or sharper wines to taste unhappily acidic and sour, but a spicy, buttery "Gewürz" will bring the menu's combination of sweet and savoury to life.

0:00 Be thankful that in 1 hour, you'll be out of the kitchen with nothing left to do but receive praise for your fine cooking.

0:01 Arrange the oven racks so you can put the ham on the bottom rack and the pie on the top rack. Preheat oven to 425°F (220°C). Remove the pie shell from the freezer. Coarsely chop the squash, ½ onion and apple into 1½-inch (4-cm) pieces and place them in a saucepan with enough chicken stock to cover. Bring the mixture to a boil. Reduce heat and let simmer 30 minutes or until the squash is softened.

0:10 Place the ham in a large roasting pan. Drizzle ¼ cup (50 mL) maple syrup over its surface. Peel and quarter two onions. Peel the garlic cloves. Wash the new and sweet potatoes; cut the sweet potato into 1½-inch (4 cm) cubes. Combine the onions, garlic and new and sweet potatoes with the figs, cranberries, carrots and chestnuts in a large bowl. Toss with olive oil, butter, sage, salt and pepper to taste. Add the mixture to roasting pan, cover it and place in the oven.

0:20 In a small bowl, whip 1 cup (250 mL) whipping cream with vanilla until soft peaks form. Refrigerate half for the pie topping. In a medium bowl, whisk the eggs and brown sugar together until smooth. Whisk in the pumpkin, nutmeg and liqueur. Fold in remaining whipped cream. Set aside.

0:30 Check the squash. When it's tender, purée the squash mixture in food processor until it's smooth. Stir in ⅓ cup (75 mL) whipping cream and salt and pepper to taste. Return the purée to a clean saucepan over low heat. Keep it warm until you're ready to serve it.

0:40 Drizzle ¼ cup (50 mL) maple syrup over ham and stir vegetables. Re-cover them.

0:45 Pour the pumpkin into the pie shell and place it on a baking sheet on the top rack of oven. Set the timer for 45 minutes.

0:55 If there is room, place the soup bowls in the oven for a few minutes to warm them. Serve the soup with a dollop of crème fraîche.

0:60 Lower heat to 350°F (180°C). When you are ready to serve the main course, remove the ham and vegetables from the oven. The pie is baked when a knife inserted in the filling comes out clean. Serve pumpkin pie warm with a dollop of whipped cream.

Squash and Apple Soup with Crème Fraîche

1 lb (500 g) peeled squash
½ onion
1 apple, peeled and cored
3½ to 4 cups (875 mL to 1 L) chicken stock
⅓ cup (75 mL) whipping cream
⅓ cup (75 mL) crème fraîche or sour cream
Sea salt and fresh pepper

Maple-Glazed Ham with Autumn Fruits and Vegetables

2 to 3 lb (1 to 1.5 kg) boneless cured and smoked ham
½ cup (125 mL) maple syrup
2 small onions
8 cloves garlic
12 small new potatoes
1 large sweet potato
1 cup (250 mL) fresh figs (4 to 6), halved
½ cup (125 mL) fresh or frozen cranberries
1 lb (500 g) prepeeled baby carrots
8 shelled chestnuts or 16 shelled hazelnuts
3 tbsp (45 mL) olive oil
3 tbsp (45 mL) butter, cut into small pieces
8 sprigs sage
⅛ tsp (0.5 mL) sea salt
Fresh pepper

Pumpkin Pie with White Chocolate Liqueur

1 9-in (23-cm) frozen pie shell
1 cup (250 mL) whipping cream
¼ tsp (1 mL) vanilla extract
3 eggs
⅓ cup (75 mL) brown sugar
2 cups (500 mL) canned pumpkin
½ tsp (2 mL) freshly grated nutmeg
¼ cup (50 mL) white chocolate liqueur

MENU FOR FOUR

Ceviche

Fiesta Chicken Mole

Celebration Rice

Mango y Carambola

El Día de los Muertos means the Day of the Dead and is the Mexican version of All Souls' Day. This major fiesta welcomes home the souls of each family's relatives and honours them with flowers, decorations and altars laden with gifts. Food is prepared for the whole family, those living and those who have moved into the spirit world. This menu brings a taste of this Mexican fiesta to Canada.

THAT LATIN BEAT

The complex and subtle flavouring of Mexican culinary tradition is a palatable delight.

Mexican food, like so many cuisines, has suffered at the hands of Anglo interpretation. TexMex chains serving canned, mashed beans and cheddar certainly have their appeal for those needing a bite on the run but that food bears as much resemblance to Latin cuisine as hamburgers do to filet mignon. The complex and subtle flavouring—the balance of spice and seasoning that constitutes real Mexican culinary tradition, with its many regional variations—is a palatable delight that Canadians are happily becoming more familiar with through travel, beautiful cookbooks and the authentic Hispanic restaurants that are opening up across the country.

In Latin America, it is common to be served ceviche, or cebiche, as an appetizer or tapas. Tapas are small dishes of piquant food, ideally suited to enjoy while sipping a drink on a patio or open-air café, as the bowl perches perfectly on a glass of beer or wine, thus keeping out any uninvited flying guests. Ceviche should always be made with the freshest seafood because although the lime juice firms up the flesh of the fish and transforms it to an opaque colour, the fish is not actually cooked. Dress up your ceviche with chopped tomatoes or peppers or complement the sharp taste of lime with your favourite herbs or spices. The avocado shell is a fanciful touch that works wonderfully with the lime and olive oil.

When writing my *Nice Timing* columns, I look for great classical dishes that will withstand a good deal of simplification. The end result cannot hope to have the intricate balance of flavours of the original dish, which often takes hours or days to prepare. I am happy, though, to create something that can be quickly assembled but retains the essence of the original dish. I have a lot of nerve calling this menu's main course a mole. Traditionally, a mole is a work of time-consuming care and passion, involving a perfect mix of roasted chilies and spices, ground to a paste in a mortar. There are numerous versions of this dish; the state of Oaxaca alone claims seven different types identified by the type of local chili used in the sauce. All this being said, I still enjoy this yummy approximation of the Mexican festival dish, with its unusual and satisfying blend of spices and chocolate. As I sit in my office, snacking on Hershey's Kisses, I hope my fellow chocoholics will understand the thrill I feel when given the excuse to add chocolate to anything—even chicken.

Many Mexican desserts, those fantastically sweet, concentrated custards, flans, pastes and candies, were originally devised by Spanish convent nuns with more time on their hands than I. For a fast dessert that still has a Hispanic beat, nothing is easier than combining luscious southern fruits with a little *helados*. I have discovered, to my delight, a great cheat for dressing up desserts. Melt a little ice cream and use it as you would crème anglais to mask a dessert plate or set a small cake in.

This menu is not a sommelier's best-case scenario by far. There are many flavours to marry here, from the combination of lime, garlic, vinegar and cilantro in the first course to the chili and chocolate of the mole. There are brilliant tastes exploding from this meal. My choice for sipping alongside this celebration dinner is a very crisp (fittingly) New World Sauvignon Blanc.

0:00 Okay, I admit it. I'm cheating. But believe me, you'll love the ceviche so much, you'll forgive me. So the night before this dinner, cut the snapper into 1-inch (2.5-cm) cubes. Watch for any small bones that might not have been removed. Combine the lime juice, garlic, cilantro, vinegar and bay leaf. Pour over the snapper in a glass or stainless steel bowl. Cover with plastic wrap and refrigerate overnight.

0:01 *For the chicken:* Remove most of the skin from the chicken. It's all right to leave the skin that is more difficult to remove, like around the legs. Lightly season the chicken with salt and pepper. Cut the onion into thin slices and cook them in oil, over medium high heat, until they are soft. Chop the garlic and chilies and add them to the onion. Stir in the remaining flavourings to make a paste. Add the chicken pieces, coat them in the paste and brown them as much as possible without burning the paste. Cover with 2 cups (500 mL) water, add the cinnamon and bring to a boil. Reduce the heat to simmer and cook, covered, for 25 minutes. Remove the lid and cook for an additional 10 minutes. Let the chicken continue to cook over a low heat until you are ready to serve it, when the sauce can be thickened if necessary.

0:20 While the chicken is cooking, prepare the rice: Wash it in cold water until the water runs clear. Dice the onion and carrot. Chop the garlic. In an oven-safe pot with a tight-fitting lid, cook the onions and carrot in oil over medium high heat until they are soft. Stir in the garlic and rice. Coat the rice with oil. Add 3 cups (750 mL) water and the peas, and bring it all to a boil. Cover the pot and place it in oven for 20 minutes. When the rice is ready, remove it from oven, fluff it with a fork and keep it covered to stay warm until service.

0:40 *For dessert:* Remove the ice cream from the freezer to melt. Place shortcake cups on individual dessert plates and drizzle them with ½ tbsp (2 mL) corn syrup each. Cut the mango into ¼-inch (6-mm) slices and arrange them so they fan out of the shortcake. Set the dishes aside.

0:50 *To serve ceviche:* Cut the avocados in half lengthwise to make two cups. Taste the ceviche and add salt and pepper to taste. Place the ceviche in the avocado cups. Drizzle with olive oil and serve.

0:60 When you are ready to serve the chicken, remove the pieces from the pan, and remove and discard the cinnamon. Reduce the sauce over a high heat until it reaches the desired thickness, then salt and pepper it to taste. Place the chicken pieces on a bed of rice and cover them with sauce. If desired, garnish the plate with fresh chopped cilantro.

To finish the dessert: Spoon melted ice cream onto the plates around the shortbread. Top the mango with 2 tbsp (25 mL) sorbet and garnish with carambola and mint leaves.

Ceviche

½ lb (250 g) fresh boned, skinned red snapper
½ cup (125 mL) lime juice (about 3 limes)
2 cloves garlic
2 tbsp (25 mL) cilantro
¼ cup (50 mL) shallot vinegar
1 bay leaf
2 avocados
Sea salt and fresh pepper
1 tbsp (15 mL) olive oil

Fiesta Chicken Mole

1 small chicken, cut into eight pieces (2 to 3 lbs/1 to 1.25 kg)
Sea salt and fresh pepper
2 tbsp (25 mL) oil
1 onion
4 cloves garlic
1 poblano chili
2 jalapeño chilies
1 cinnamon stick
¼ cup (50 mL) sesame seeds
¼ cup (50 mL) almonds
2 tbsp (25 mL) cocoa
2 tbsp (25 mL) sugar
2 cups (500 mL) cold water

Celebration Rice

1 ½ cups (375 mL) basmati rice
1 small onion
1 carrot
2 cloves garlic
¼ cup (50 mL) vegetable oil
1 cup (250 mL) frozen peas

Mango y Carambola

½ cup (125 mL) vanilla ice cream
4 shortcake cups
2 tbsp (25 mL) corn syrup
1 mango
½ cup (125 mL) mango sorbet
1 carambola (star fruit), sliced
8 mint leaves

MENU FOR TWO

Warm Pear and Bacon Salad

Steak Frites

Iced Vacherin

I am a French fry junkie. To my mind, crisp golden strips of potatoes are the perfect indulgence. But let's face it, this fast food is a nutritional nightmare. Still, I won't, I can't— please don't ask me to—give it up.

FRITES, ALORS!

The quest for the perfect frite, that fabulous French fry, is fraught with pitfalls.

French fries steal the show in this month's bistro menu, which begins with a bitter endive and frisée salad, tamed with a pear and bacon dressing. The salad leads into that bistro classic, steak frites. For dessert we offer a 5-minute version of vacherin glacé, meringue nests filled with ice cream.

The quest for the perfect frite, that fabulous French fry, crispy and golden on the outside, soft and mealy moist on the inside, is fraught with pitfalls. Moisture, the sugar and starch content of the potato, the variety of oil and the temperature for frying must be just right to ensure success.

To get the scientific skinny on the correct oil temperature for frying potatoes, I spoke to Dr. Rick Yada, who is chair of the Food Sciences Department at the University of Guelph. Yada informed me that cooking fries at a higher temperature quickly evaporates the potato's moisture content and cooks and seals the outer layer of the potato, preventing excess fat absorption, which is preferable if you are watching your calories. However, if your first concern is taste and texture, I recommend blanching potatoes at a lower temperature to cook them through, in the process absorbing oil and retaining moisture, which gives them a soft interior.

Professional kitchens swear by the blanching method: Cut potatoes are deep-fried in oil at a low temperature (225°F to 325°F/110°C to 160°C) until tender. Parcooked potatoes are then set aside to drain while the oil heats up. When the temperature reaches 375°F (190°C), the fries are quickly cooked until their exterior is golden brown and crispy. Variations on this theme can be found in most cookbooks. Yet when I spoke to home cooks, they invariably cooked their fries once at a high temperature and were satisfied with the results.

If you cook your fries only once, cut the potatoes as thinly as possible to ensure that they cook inside and out.

A final word: You may wonder why we call frites "French fries." The reason has nothing to do with their country of origin. Rather, the name comes from the fact that the potato is frenched, or cut into thin strips, before frying. *Voilà! C'est magnifique.*

0:00 Open a bottle of New World Merlot and make a toast to the chef.

0:01 Peel the potatoes and slice them lengthwise into thin sticks. Rinse the potatoes, then cover them with very cold water. If you have a deep fryer, add canola oil to the minimum level; otherwise, pour 3 cups (750 mL) oil into a pot with high sides. (The hot oil will bubble up.) Clip a thermometer to the side of the pot to measure the oil temperature. Heat the oil to 225°F (110°C).

0:10 For the salad, separate and coarsely chop the endive; tear the frisée into bite-size pieces. Place them in a stainless steel bowl and set it aside. Peel and core the pear. Cut it into ½-inch (1-cm) cubes. Set them aside.

0:15 *To prepare the vacherin:* Use a spoon to gently scrape out the bottoms of two meringue rings. Do not try to cut them out or the meringue will crumble. Place the bottomless rings on top of two whole rings, making two meringue nests with high sides. Crumble the cut-out meringue and mix 2 tbsp (25 mL) meringue crumbs with chopped almonds. Place 1 tbsp (15 mL) vanilla ice cream in the centre of each nest and press it firmly into the bottom. Top each nest with strawberry ice cream. The ice cream should fill the centre of the nest; add more if necessary. Sprinkle with the crumbled meringue and almond mixture, and set the nests in the freezer until shortly before you serve them. In a small skillet over medium heat, melt the butter. Add the shallots and sauté them several minutes or until they're soft. Set them aside.

0:30 *To blanch the potatoes:* Drain the potatoes and pat them dry to prevent sputtering. Carefully drop the potatoes into oil, using a fry basket if you have one. Blanch until they're soft, 5 to 7 minutes. Remove the potatoes from the oil, using a wide slotted spoon if you don't have a fry basket. Drain off the excess oil and set the potatoes aside. Remove the pot of oil from the heat temporarily.

0:40 *To prepare the steak:* Butterfly the pieces of steak by slicing them horizontally without cutting through to the opposite side, so the steak opens like a book. Score each piece by slicing a grid pattern over the surface, ¼ inch (6 mm) deep. Pound each steak flat. Season them with salt and pepper and brush one side with ½ tbsp (7 mL) mustard. Set the meat aside.

0:50 *For the salad:* Cut the bacon into ¼- to ½-inch (6-mm to 1-cm) pieces. Place a medium skillet over a medium-high heat. Add the bacon and fry it until it begins to crisp. Pour off the excess fat. Add the

Mixed Grain Salad, p. 75

Warm Scallop Salad, p. 43

Portobello Mushroom Tower on Orzo with Truffle Oil, p. 59

Prosciutto and Smoked Turkey Wraps, p. 67

Coconut Curried Shrimp, p. 11

T-Bone Tails with Peppercorn Sauce, p. 95

Skewered Capon Breasts, p. 75

Gingered Cherries Jubilee, p. 75

pear and sauté it until it is lightly browned, but not too soft. Add the vinegar, scraping up any brown bits from bottom of pan. Remove the pan from the heat and stir in the olive oil. Season the endive and frisée lightly with salt and pepper, then toss with the warm dressing. Divide the salad between two plates; serve it immediately. Return the deep-frying oil to heat; raise the temperature to 375°F (190°C).

After you have enjoyed your salad, add the fries to the hot oil until they're crisp and golden, 7 to 9 minutes. Drain them on a paper towel and sprinkle with salt. Meanwhile, cook the steaks in separate skillets over high heat, mustard side up, for 3 minutes. Flip the steaks, then brush the tops with mustard. Cook for an additional 3 to 4 minutes. Serve the steak with the shallots and frites. Five to 10 minutes before serving, remove the vacherins from the freezer to let them soften slightly.

Warm Pear and Bacon Salad

1 head Belgian endive
1 handful frisée or curly endive
1 pear
2 slices bacon
1 tbsp (15 mL) shallot vinegar or red wine vinegar
1 tbsp (15 mL) olive oil
Sea salt and fresh pepper

Steak Frites

2 medium baking potatoes
3 cups (750 mL) canola or peanut oil
2 tsp (10 mL) butter
¼ cup (50 mL) chopped shallots
2 pieces (each 6 oz/170 g) flank steak
Sea salt and fresh pepper
2 tbsp (25 mL) coarse-grained mustard

Iced Vacherin

4 store-bought meringue rings
2 tbsp (25 mL) chopped almonds
2 tbsp (25 mL) vanilla ice cream
2 tbsp (25 mL) strawberry ice cream

MENU FOR TWO

Smoked Mackerel
with Red Onion and Capers

Paella

Bananas in Custard
and Chocolate

KISS. Keep it simple and smart. This is an old, hackneyed bit of business wisdom that means that to have the best chance of success, a project should be as uncomplicated as possible. The smaller the number of variables, the less the chance of a meltdown or a SNAFU. Do a simple thing—do it well. This appetizer applies both maxims. Some sour cream, a little fish and a touch of garnish combine in a few minutes to make an tasty nibble worthy of a place at table.

A MACKEREL A DAY

The salty little anchovy adds a dimension of taste to paella that is magnificent.

Mackerel is one of those cold-water, fatty fish that health food gurus have been raving about. It contains high quantities of omega-3 fatty acids, which are reported to possess a panoply of health benefits. The U.S. National Library of Medicine has an online research site called PubMed, where it is possible to find peer-reviewed journal articles relating to all the newest research in the field of medicine. At the time of this writing, there are 3,771 journal articles related to omega-3 fatty acids. The Center for Genetics, Nutrition and Health in Washington, D.C., reports that these fatty acids have been shown to be beneficial in the prevention of coronary heart disease, hypertension, diabetes, arthritis, colitis, Crohn's disease and pulmonary disease. There are other articles reporting positive effects in everything from the suppression of breast cancer to weight loss. The Mayo Clinic puts it succinctly in their article, saying, "Make fish a regular on your plate."

Paella is a Spanish dish named for the *paellera*, the wide, shallow pan that it is cooked in. If your kitchen complement does not include this two-handled pan, an oven-safe frying pan will do. I don't recommend a nonstick pan, as the mussels could scratch it. You will, however, be less inclined to eat the finished dish directly out of your frying pan than out of the paellera, as is the custom.

Ode to a Small Fish: "I think that I shall never see, This thing: a lovely anchovy." Really, not a pretty fish, but as my mother's kitchen staples included bread, butter, milk and eggs, mine include anchovies. These salty little *poissons* pack a powerful punch and are indispensable flavour builders. They add a dimension of taste to paella that is magnificent for its levels of flavour. The taste of onion, on garlic, on anchovy, on seafood, on meat and good broth, all lend their goodness to saffron-scented basmati rice.

Originally I wanted to suggest Banana Cream Pie for this menu but I felt it would be asking too much to make paella and pie in 1 hour. While paella is actually incredibly straightforward to prepare, there are a number of ingredients to assemble and chop, and this can become time consuming. So I simplified the dessert by serving instead bananas in chocolate cups with store-bought custard. When time allows, I prefer to make my own CUSTARD by scalding 1 cup (250 mL) milk and ½ cup (125 mL) cream with one split vanilla pod. Meanwhile, whisk together 3 egg yolks and ½ cup (125 mL) sugar until it is pale yellow and ribbony. Slowly whisk the hot milk into the eggs and return the mixture to a medium heat. Stir constantly until the custard becomes thick. Pass it through a thin strainer to remove any lumps and refrigerate, covered with plastic wrap. The custard will become thicker as it cools.

CATHERINE'S WINE TIP

Here I have to recommend a traditional Old World Pinot Blanc from Alsace for its tones of lichee and lemon.

0:00 Feeling blue? Yet another grey November day? Never fret: a savoury meal with soul-restoring qualities is just 1 hour away.

0:01 *To assemble the mackerel:* Spoon 1 tbsp (15 mL) sour cream onto the centre of each appetizer plate. Slice the mackerel fillet along centre crease. Cut each piece into three diamond-shaped pieces. Arrange the pieces in a star pattern over the sour cream. Cover with red onion rings and capers.

0:10 *For the dessert:* Spoon 1 tbsp (15 mL) custard into each chocolate cup. Slice the banana over the custard. Spoon the remaining custard over the banana. Whip the cream in a narrow container until it is stiff, adding the sugar just before the cream is fully whipped. Set both aside in the refrigerator and garnish the custard with whipped cream just before service.

0:20 *To make the paella:* Set the stock and tomatoes in a small saucepan, with the saffron, over a medium heat to warm and infuse. Heat the oil over a medium-high heat in a paellera or, failing that, a large frying pan. Chop the onion and cook it in the oil until it is soft. Mince the garlic and anchovy and add them to the onion, along with the dried chilies. Cut the sausage and chicken into 1-inch (2.5-cm) pieces and brown them in the oil. Rinse the rice in cold water until the water runs clear and stir the rice into the pan. Add salt to the stock and pour it over the rice.

Bring it to a boil, cover and place the pan in a hot oven for 10 minutes. When 10 minutes are up, add the mussels (see page 113 for notes on shellfish safety), shrimp and peas, season with pepper, and return the pan to the oven, covered for an additional 10 to 15 minutes or until the mussels have all opened, the shrimp has turned pink on the outside and white on the inside, and the rice is tender but firm to the bite. Add pepper and serve.

Smoked Mackerel with Red Onion and Capers

2 tbsp (25 mL) sour cream
4 oz (120 g) smoked, peppered mackerel fillet (1 large fillet)
8 large rings red onion
2 tbsp (25 mL) capers

Paella

1⅓ cups (325 mL) chicken stock
4 canned plum tomatoes
Pinch saffron
3 tbsp (45 mL) olive oil
½ small onion
3 cloves garlic
2 anchovies
¼ tsp (1 mL) dried chilies
3 oz (90 g) pork sausage
3 oz (90 g) boneless, skinless chicken breast
⅔ cups (150 mL) basmati rice
¼ tsp (1 mL) sea salt
18 cultured mussels, washed and debearded
5 oz (150 g) large shrimp, peeled and deveined
⅓ cup (75 mL) frozen peas, thawed
Fresh pepper

Bananas in Custard and Chocolate

6 tbsp (90 mL) canned Devon custard
2 chocolate cups
1 banana
⅓ cup (75 mL) whipping cream
½ tsp (2 mL) sugar

MENU FOR TWO

Asian Coleslaw

Steamed Pickerel in
Black Bean Sauce

Rice Noodles

Fried Plantain

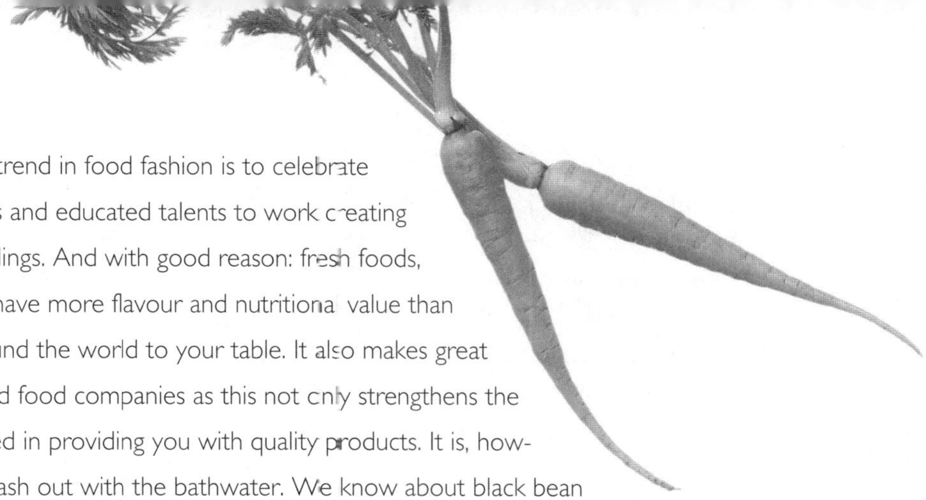

Shop locally; eat globally. The current trend in food fashion is to celebrate local foods. To put sharpened palates and educated talents to work creating dishes in harmony with regional surroundings. And with good reason: fresh foods, grown and produced nearby will always have more flavour and nutritional value than something that has travelled halfway around the world to your table. It also makes great sense to support local farmers, bakers and food companies as this not only strengthens the economy but also keeps people interested in providing you with quality products. It is, however, unnecessary to throw the baby squash out with the bathwater. We know about black bean sauces, ginger root, coriander and Asian pear, and there's no sense trying to keep us down on the farm now that we've tasted sashimi. The point is to take a local product, like pickerel, and dress it up with something tasty like black bean sauce. And if you're living in Canada under that unmistakable November sky, the time for fresh local produce is past. Since you're eating bananas anyway, why not try the occasional plantain?

THAT UNMISTAKABLE NOVEMBER SKY

If you're living in Canada, under a November sky, the time for fresh local produce is past.

Asian pear tops a crisp combination of raw veggies for our first course. The nijisseiki pear is grown in Japan and has found a welcome home in my repertoire of international fruits. The flesh is white, very crisp and with a light sweetness that lends itself to eating raw. Michihili cabbage, commonly known as Chinese cabbage, makes a wonderful slaw mixed with grated carrot and tossed in a dressing that commingles the sweet and salty flavours that characterize many Asian dishes. Unlike traditional coleslaw, this version does not lend itself to marinating for a long time as the thinner cabbage leaves become soggy and unappealing

A ripe plantain is not a thing of beauty. Black and soft, sometimes shrivelled and sticky to touch, it takes a stout heart to approach it for the first time. A good rule of thumb is to leave it until you think it must have finally gone bad, wait 2 more days, then cook it. Green and yellow plantains are used in Latin cookery, but at that stage they are very starchy and are boiled and eaten as a vegetable. As the fruit ripens, the starches turn to sugar and the sweetness comes out. This flavour is intensified and shown to its best advantage when plantains are fried in butter. And, of course, a rum sauce never hurts.

> **CATHERINE'S WINE TIP**
>
> *Well, there are many flavours to match here. After much assessment, I think that chilled sake comes up a winner. I love this rice wine, and its evenness and consistency are ideal with this menu. An Asian beer is my second choice, but somehow beans and beer seem to distract from the theme.*

0:00 Short, dark days can lead to gloomy spirits. Treat yourself to some small indulgence. Good chocolate. A fine brandy. Send yourself some flowers or dance with your cat—whatever makes you happy.

0:01 *To prepare the coleslaw:* Julienne the cabbage and grate the carrot. Whisk together the remaining ingredients. Toss the cabbage and carrot in the dressing and set them aside. When you're ready to serve the coleslaw, drain and place it on two appetizer plates. Grate the pear and serve it on top of the slaw. Both the noodles and fish are best if served immediately after cooking, so I like to have the coleslaw as the second course. Its crisp, fresh flavours are perfect after the savoury saltiness of the other dishes.

0:15 *For the plantain:* Leaving the skin on, cut the plantain in half so you have two even-sized, fully round pieces. Then slice each piece horizontally to yield three strips. Then, carefully, remove the skin. Keeping the skin on during cutting helps the fruit maintain its shape. Fry the strips in 1 tbsp (15 mL) butter over a medium high heat until they are browned on both sides, about 5 minutes. If necessary, use more butter. At the same time, in a separate pan cook the sugar in 1 tbsp (15 mL) butter over a high heat until it begins to turn golden—do not stir. Remove it from heat and carefully stir in 1 tbsp (15 mL) rum. This might flame for a second. Let the mixture cool for 2 minute, then stir in 1 tbsp (15 mL) cream. Set the plantain and sauce aside but keep them in their pans. When you're ready to serve the plantain, place the pans over a high heat until they're just warmed. Serve the plantain with ice cream and drizzle the sauce over top.

0:30 *For the pickerel and noodles:* Immerse the rice noodles in warm water and leave them to soak. Place 2 cups (500 mL) water in the bottom of a steamer and put it on to boil. Cut the ginger root into ¼-inch (6-mm) slices and drop them in the water. Cut the pickerel fillet into two even-sized pieces and rub in the black bean sauce. Mince the onion and garlic. Heat the oil in a large skillet and sauté the onions and garlic over a high heat until they're soft. Add ½ cup (125 mL) water and bring it to a boil; then toss in the noodles and cook them until the water is evaporated and the noodles are soft, about 3 to 5 minutes. Remove the pan from the heat and toss the noodles in the remaining ingredients.

Place the fish on a steaming rack and steam, covered, for 10 minutes per inch (2.5 cm). If you don't have a steamer, make a rack of chopsticks over a medium-sized pot to hold the fish above the steam and cover with a deep lid. Serve the fish on the noodles and garnish with whole stems of fresh coriander.

Asian Coleslaw

2 leaves Chinese cabbage

1 carrot

1 Asian pear

2 tsp (10 mL) lemon juice

1 tbsp (15 mL) mango juice

1 tbsp (15 mL) canola oil

½ tsp (2 mL) soy sauce

Steamed Pickerel in Black Bean Sauce

1 lb (500 g) pickerel fillet

2-inch (5-cm) piece ginger root

1 tbsp (15 mL) black bean sauce

Rice Noodles

6 oz (170 g) broad rice noodles

¼ onion

2 cloves garlic

2 tbsp (15 mL) canola oil

¼ cup (50 mL) fresh coriander

2 tsp (10 mL) sesame oil

1 tsp (5 mL) garlic chili sauce

Fried Plantain

1 very ripe plantain

2 tbsp (25 mL) butter

1 tbsp (15 mL) sugar

1 tbsp (15 mL) rum

1 tbsp (15 mL) cream

½ cup (125 mL) vanilla ice cream

WINTER

And in winter, when you draw the wine,
Let there be in your heart a song for each cup;
And let there be in the song a remembrance for the autumn days,
And for the vineyard, and for the winepress.

–*Kahlil Gibran,* The Prophet

One of the best things about this section is that it contains not one but two recipes for chocolate. Although both are tantalizing, the chocolate soufflé is my favourite. It completes a black-tie New Year's menu of oysters on the half shell and roasted Cornish hens. To counterbalance the excesses of the season, I've also suggested a low-fat menu, which is built around an elegant salmon *en papillote.* As I write this, it is dusk and the first snow has fallen. My neighbour's children head out with their toboggan for an early evening ride. The world seems to me a peaceful place made all the more comforting by good food and the sweet anticipation of the entertaining season.

January and February are ideal months for wrapping yourself in the warm cocoon of your kitchen and preparing comfort food, which has been defined as "anything anyone's grandma would cook." At its best, comfort food is heartwarming stews and full-flavoured dishes like Coq au Vin, Cottage Pie, or Bread and Butter Pudding.

MENU FOR TWO

Oysters on the Half Shell

Cornish Hens with Pomegranate and Blood Orange

Wild Rice and Green Beans

Chocolate Soufflé

Simplicity and elegance are the keys to the ideal New Year's Eve dinner. The last meal of the year demands more than a little panache, but time is still of the essence—most cooks will have plans to be out of the kitchen well before the clock strikes midnight.

A MEAL TO REMEMBER

Indulge and serve champagne with a cube of sugar, a drop of bitters and a teaspoon of brandy.

Oysters on the half shell have long been considered a delicacy. They must be served within an hour or two of opening. Although oyster shucking is not difficult, it does take some practice. For this reason, I suggest the inexperienced open their oysters before they start to prepare the rest of the meal. Better yet, ask your dining partner to do it while you prepare the rest of the meal.

To shuck oysters, do not use a regular knife, which might break, possibly injuring you and fatally wounding a good knife. Instead, buy an inexpensive oyster knife; its short, broad blade is sturdy enough to pop open a shell and its hand guard offers some protection from the oyster's sharp exterior.

Before shucking, use a stiff brush to scrub off grit and dirt from the shells under cold running water. Once they are thoroughly cleaned, wrap a shell flat side up in a tea towel, leaving the pointed, hinged end of the oyster accessible. Carefully insert the blade into the shell's hinge and twist to separate the two shell halves. Lift off the top shell, sliding the knife inside to separate the oyster meat from the top shell. Break off and discard the top shell, trying not to spill the liquor in the bottom half. Carefully run the knife underneath the oyster to release it from the bottom and remove any visible bits of shell or debris from the meat and liquor.

Cornish hens taste like chicken but their presentation allows much more flair. A single small roasted bird served on a bed of wild rice with ruby pomegranate seeds and juicy blood oranges for garnish simply can't be beat for visual appeal. The sweet spice of ginger marmalade rubbed into the skin makes a delicious glaze.

The secret to soufflé, this month's dessert, is to beat the egg whites properly. Whipping the whites in a copper-lined bowl works best, but a stainless steel or glass bowl will do. Clean the beaters of an electric mixer and a non-plastic bowl first with vinegar, then rinse well with plenty of cold water before adding the eggs, which have been brought to room temperature. Many an egg white has failed to reach its desired volume because of a trace of oil, grease or detergent. Begin beating slowly, then increase speed. Stop when the whites are stiff and cling to beaters. Do not overmix: If you do, the egg whites will not hold their air through the cooking process.

On New Year's Eve, indulging a penchant for bubbly is a time-honoured tradition. Before dinner, serve this tempting CHAMPAGNE COCKTAIL: Place 1 cube sugar, 1 tsp (5 mL) brandy and a few drops of Angostura Bitters in the bottom of each flute and top with Champagne. Serve immediately; the Champagne cocktail, like the soufflé, loses its character in a breath. Champagne has the reputation of being the perfect accompaniment to every course. I am not the one to argue this point, but if you would rather have something a little less effervescent with your entrée, try a fruity Beaujolais.

0:00 Serve a round of Champagne cocktails before you start cooking.

0:01 Put a bottle of peppered vodka in the freezer. Cut the lemon into wedges. Preheat the oven to 375°F (190°C). Remove the seeds from the pomegranate by quartering it and using your fingers or a small spoon to separate them from the membrane. Peel the orange, if desired. Cut four thin slices, and then cube the remainder. Set aside half the pomegranate seeds and the orange slices for garnish. Rinse the hens, pat them dry and stuff them with the chopped orange and half the pomegranate seeds. Rub ½ tsp (2 mL) butter over each hen and sprinkle them lightly with salt and pepper. Rub each with half the ginger marmalade.

0:15 Place the hens in a shallow roasting pan on a rack in the middle of the oven. Set the timer for 45 minutes. For the green beans, place 4 cups (1 L) water and ½ tsp (2 mL) salt in a saucepan over medium-high heat. For the wild rice, combine the stock and ¼ tsp (1 mL) salt in another saucepan over medium-high heat on a back burner. Place crushed ice in two shallow serving bowls. Nestle the shucked oysters on half shells in the crushed ice. Refrigerate them until serving.

0:30 Rinse the wild rice and add it to boiling stock. Return it to a boil, stir, then cover and let simmer 30 to 45 minutes or until the kernels are soft and outer shells have exploded. Wash the green beans and remove the stems. To blanch the beans, drop them in boiling salted water and cook until they are just tender, approximately 5 minutes. Remove the beans with a slotted spoon and rinse them under very cold water; set them aside.

0:40 Butter two 1-cup (250-mL) soufflé dishes and dust them with granulated sugar. Prepare a roux by combining 1 tsp (5 mL) each butter and flour in a heavy-bottomed saucepan over a medium heat. Stir with a wooden spoon until the roux turns pale golden.

Add the cold milk and whisk until the mixture is smooth and thickened. Remove the saucepan from the heat and stir in the chocolate chips until they're melted. Stir in the egg yolks one at a time. In a copper, stainless steel or glass bowl, combine the egg whites, salt and cream of tartar. Using an electric mixer, beat at low speed until soft peaks form. Increase the speed to medium and beat in 1 tsp (5 mL) sugar until the whites cling to the beaters. Gently fold a quarter of the whites into the chocolate mixture. Fold in the remaining whites. Divide between two soufflé dishes, cover with plastic wrap and refrigerate.

0:60 Check the hens: Insert a knife or meat thermometer into an inner thigh; when the liquid runs clear or the temperature reads 170°F (77°C), they are done. Let them rest, covered, until you are ready to serve them. Remove the rice from the heat, drain if necessary and keep it covered until the main course is served. Pour 1 tsp (5 mL) peppered vodka over each oyster and serve with lemon wedges.

Between the first and main courses, reheat the beans by placing 1 tbsp (15 mL) butter in a skillet over a medium heat. When it has melted, add the beans and sauté them until they're hot. Lightly season them with salt and pepper to taste. Serve with the wild rice and Cornish hens garnished with the reserved blood orange slices and pomegranate seeds.

Soufflé is best served directly from the oven; put the soufflé dishes in the oven on the bottom rack after you finish your entrée. Bake for 15 minutes. Serve the soufflé immediately, dusted with icing sugar, if desired.

Oysters on the Half Shell

3 tbsp (45 mL) peppered vodka
1 lemon
Crushed ice
12 freshly shucked oysters (see introduction for shucking instructions)

Cornish Hens with Pomegranate and Blood Orange

1 pomegranate
1 blood orange, unpeeled
2 small Cornish hens (1 ½ lb/750 g each)
1 tsp (5 mL) butter
Sea salt and fresh pepper
2 tbsp (25 mL) ginger marmalade

Wild Rice

4 cups (1 L) chicken stock
¼ tsp (1 mL) sea salt
¾ cup (175 mL) wild rice

Green Beans

4 cups (1 L) water
½ tsp (2 mL) sea salt
6 oz (170 g) green beans
1 tbsp (15 mL) butter
Sea salt and fresh pepper

Chocolate Soufflé

1 tsp (5 mL) all-purpose flour
1 tsp (5 mL) butter
¼ cup (50 mL) whole milk, cold
3 oz (90 g) chocolate chips
2 egg yolks
3 egg whites, at room temperature
Pinch salt
Pinch cream of tartar
1 tsp (5 mL) granulated sugar

MENU FOR TWO

Fish Soup with
Pickerel Quenelles

Salmon en Papillote

Carrot and Zucchini Ribbons

Baked Apples with Cranberries

On the twelfth day of Christmas, my true love sent to me twelve turkeys basting, eleven trifles setting, ten hams a-glazing, nine puddings steaming, eight cookies baking, seven eggs a-nogging, six geese a-stuffing, five coated figs, four pecan pies, three frenched hens, two chocolate cakes and a partridge in a pear coulis.

ALL GOOD THINGS IN MODERATION

Baking fish en papillote *is a delicious, elegant, low-fat cooking method.*

No wonder I put on weight over the holidays. But this holiday menu substitutes lower-fat cooking methods wherever possible. It offers subtly flavoured quenelles poached in fish broth, tender salmon steamed in parchment paper and baked apples tarted up with cranberries.

Quenelles are dumplings made from ground fish, veal, chicken or vegetables. Traditionally, they are prepared with butter and lots of cream, whereas this version is bound with just a little whipped cream.

Making the soup for this menu, I used a powdered fish bouillon for the first time in my life, with acceptable results. Of course, homemade stock is always preferred and fish stock is the quickest stock you can make.

For FISH STOCK: Place 1 lb (500 g) fish bones (not from an oily fish such as salmon or mackerel) and shellfish trimmings (such as shrimp and lobster shells) in a pot with the white part of 1 leek, 3 shallots, 1 small bunch parsley, 1 smashed garlic clove, 1 cup (250 mL) white wine and 3 cups (750 mL) cold water. Bring the mixture to a boil over high heat, then reduce the heat and simmer, uncovered, for 30 minutes, skimming off any foam that rises to the top. Strain the stock through a sieve or colander lined with cheesecloth and let the liquid cool before refrigerating. Use it as soon as possible, since fish stock will lose its flavour after a day or two.

Baking fish en papillote is a delicious and elegant low-fat cooking method. Parchment paper is sold in rolls and carried by most grocery stores. The fish is sprinkled with flavour builders such as fresh herbs and spices, then wrapped in parchment paper. When it is placed in a hot oven, the fillet steams in its package. If you don't mind the addition of a few grams of fat, dollop some butter on the fish before or after cooking.

Apple pie deserves its place as one of the great holiday favourites. However, flaky pastry cannot be obtained without adding generous amounts of fat. As a no-pastry alternative, a light sprinkle of brown sugar, cinnamon and vanilla lend their sweet charms to tender baked apples and tart cranberries. The result is a dessert so virtuous that I could not resist adding just a touch of ice cream.

0:00 Deck the halls with boughs of holly and open a bottle of Chablis.

0:01 *For the quenelles:* Run your finger along the top of the pickerel fillet to check for bones, which can be removed with tweezers.Cut the pickerel into cubes. Purée them in a food processor until they're smooth. Add basil, 4 chives, whipped cream, bread crumbs, cayenne, nutmeg, salt and pepper. Blend until a paste is formed. Place the mixture in a bowl, then cover and refrigerate it.

0:10 *To make the apples:* Core and scoop out the centres of two apples, leaving wide-mouthed shells suitable for stuffing. Peel, core and chop remaining the apple into ¼-inch (5-mm) cubes. Sprinkle 1 tsp (5 mL) lemon juice and a pinch brown sugar over exposed flesh of each apple shell. Toss the apple cubes with the remaining sugar and lemon juice, cranberries, cinnamon and vanilla. Place this mixture in the bottom of a 4-cup (1-L) baking dish; set the shells, right side up, on top. Cover the dish with foil and set it aside.

0:25 *To prepare the salmon:* Fold each piece of parchment paper in half; use scissors to cut each folded piece into a half-heart shape. Open the parchment pieces and lay them flat on your work surface. Place one fillet on one side of each centrefold. Lightly salt the fish, then sprinkle it with lemon juice. Crush the peppercorns and gently press them onto the fillets. Lay two lemon slices on top of each fillet. Fold the parchment paper over and crimp the edges. Set the bundles aside on a baking sheet.

0:40 *For the soup:* Bring the fish stock and wine to a boil in a medium saucepan over high heat, then reduce the heat to simmer.

For the vegetable ribbons: Peel the carrot. Using a peeler, shave wide ribbons from the carrot and zucchini by firmly pressing the peeler into the vegetable and running it along the full length. Place the ribbons in a bowl, cover it and set it aside. Preheat oven to 375°F (190°C).

0:45 *To finish the soup:* Cut each of four chives into four lengths. Add the red pepper to the simmering stock. Form eight football-shaped dumplings from the chilled fish mixture. Dip two teaspoons in cold water to prevent the dough from sticking, then shape ⅛ fish mixture by firmly turning the dumplings from one spoon to the other.

0:55 Drop the chives and dumplings into the stock. Poach for 5 minutes.

0:60 Measure the thickness of the salmon and bake for 10 minutes per inch (2.5 cm); bake the apples 30 to 35 minutes.

Serve the soup. When you're ready to serve salmon, finish the vegetable ribbons: Put the orange juice in a medium saucepan. Add salt and bring the mixture to a boil. Drop in the carrots and zucchini and cook, occasionally stirring gently, for 3 minutes. Drain and serve the vegetables garnished with clementine segments. Serve the salmon in its parchment paper, so you can each unwrap a Christmas gift.

To present the dessert: Place the apple shells on individual dessert plates. Stuff each with the apple-cranberry mixture, pouring juice from pan over top. Add 1 tbsp (15 mL) ice cream to each.

Fish Soup with Pickerel Quenelles

3 oz (90 g) skinless pickerel fillet
3 leaves basil
8 chives
2 tbsp (25 mL) whipped cream or light whip topping
1 tbsp (15 mL) dry bread crumbs
Pinch cayenne
Pinch nutmeg
Pinch sea salt and white pepper
2 ½ cups (625 mL) fish stock
½ cup (125 mL) white wine
¼ red pepper, cut into strips

Salmon en Papillote

2 pieces (about 14 inch/35 cm each) parchment paper
2 salmon fillets (about 6 oz/170 g each)
Sea salt
1 tbsp (15 mL) lemon juice
2 tsp (10 mL) pink peppercorns
4 slices lemon

Carrot and Zucchini Ribbons

1 large carrot
1 large zucchini
1 cup (250 mL) orange juice
¼ tsp (1 mL) sea salt
1 clementine, in segments

Baked Apples with Cranberries

3 crispin apples
1 tbsp (15 mL) lemon juice
1 tbsp (15 mL) brown sugar
16 cranberries
½ tsp (2 mL) ground cinnamon
¼ tsp (1 mL) vanilla extract
2 tbsp (25 mL) light vanilla ice cream

MENU FOR TWO

Sautéed Chicken Livers
with White Grapes

Pepper-Crusted Beef
Tenderloin

Parmentier White
and Sweet Potatoes

Pear Crepes

You say "potayto" and I say "potahto." Or *batata*. As with the word "barbecue," we can look to the Taino people for the etymology of this common English word. *Batata* was their name for sweet potato, which made the journey to Europe in the 15th century, and was anglicized to sound like "potato." When the potato arrived from South America in the 16th century, its resemblance to the sweet potato earned the spud its moniker. But what's in a name? Nightshade, for instance, has a decidedly sinister ring to it. Particularly when prefixed by the adjective "deadly." And yet members of the nightshade family include the potato, the tomato and the eggplant. It was thus guilt by association that caused the potato to be highly suspect as a food fit for human consumption. Sir Walter Raleigh is credited with popularizing the tater in the U.K., but in France it was Antoine-Augustin Parmentier. Monsieur Parmentier enjoys the reputation of being one of the great heroes of French cuisine to this day. (And how well can anything be enjoyed by a man dead for four centuries?) He campaigned for the lowly *pomme du terre*, extolling its virtues (which he is rumoured to have discovered as a prisoner of war) and eventually he won over three stars of the day, Benjamin Franklin, Voltaire and King Louis XVI, to his culinary camp. In fact, once Louis started wearing a potato flower as an adornment, the superstitions regarding the earth apple began to dissipate. There are still many potato recipes named after its great historical supporter, including a dish of small diced potatoes sautéed in oil and tossed in parsley. I have taken the liberty of adding the *batata* for colour and variety.

PARMENTIER'S LEGACY

> *Monsieur Parmentier, a champion of the potato, is one of the great heroes of French cuisine.*

Meat is something I tend to enjoy in small quantities. Generally, I serve 3 to 4 ounces (90 to 120 g) along with plenty of grains and vegetables. So it was an exercise in pure gluttony for me to cook and happily eat the 8-oz (250-g) portion of beef tenderloin in this menu. Aptly named, this is a remarkably tender cut of meat. And dear. But then, all things in moderation, particularly moderation. If you are more inclined toward modest portions, a smaller piece of tenderloin will cook up just as nicely. Just remember to decrease the cooking time after the initial 10 minutes, as even a smaller piece of beef will benefit from searing at a high temperature. The tenderloin here is delicious simply crusted and served with horseradish mustard, but if a SAUCE will make you that much happier, try this: after removing the tenderloin, place the pan over a medium-high heat on top of the stove. Deglaze with ⅓ cup (75 mL) red wine, stirring up the bits from the bottom of the pan with a wooden spoon, and stir in 1 tsp (5 mL) horseradish mustard and 1 tbsp (15 mL) whipping cream. Reduce until the sauce coats the back of a spoon and season to taste with sea salt.

Store-bought crepes are just one of the many upscale convenience foods now available. As with everything else, there is a price paid in quality; fresh crepes simply cannot be beat. So if you do have the time, try this recipe for homemade CREPES: sift together ¼ cup (50 mL) all-purpose flour, 1 tsp (5 mL) sugar and a tiny pinch of salt. In a separate bowl, combine 1 tbsp (15 mL) melted butter with ¼ cup (50 mL) milk and 1 egg, both at room temperature. Slowly whisk the flour into the wet ingredients until the mixture is smooth; let it rest for 45 minutes. Place a nonstick or seasoned crepe pan over a medium heat. For extra buttery taste, melt ¼ tsp (1 mL) butter in the crepe pan. Spoon 3 tbsp (90 mL) batter into the pan and swirl it around to get an even coating. Let the crepe cook until it is lightly coloured on the bottom and set on the top, about 2 to 3 minutes. If you're making the crepes ahead of time, place a layer of waxed paper between each. This recipe will make four crepes, but they are smaller than the store-bought variety so use two for each serving.

CATHERINE'S WINE TIP

I've chosen a traditional Amontillado sherry to sip along with the chicken livers and white grapes. A distinctive red wine from the southwest of France, such as a slightly aged Cahors, will have enough tannin and balance suit the pepper-crusted tenderloin.

0:00 Preheat the oven to 450°F (230°C). Open the bottle and raise a glass to Parmentier. While you're at it, why not toast the farmers of Peru, the Taino people, Sir Walter Raleigh, Sir Francis Drake and Voltaire? If you are still in the mood to cook, proceed.

0:01 *To prepare the dessert:* Peel and slice the pears into very thin wedges. Place the nectar and pears in a small pan over a high heat until the liquid begins to boil. Lower the heat to simmer and reduce the juice until it has a syrupy consistency, about 15 minutes. Set it aside. While waiting for the reduction, peel the potatoes and sweet potatoes and cut them into ¼-inch (6-mm) dice.

0:20 *For the tenderloin:* Rub the tenderloin with garlic, sprinkle with salt, and rub in 1 tbsp (15 mL) mustard. Coat it with peppercorns. Place the tenderloin in a shallow baking pan in the oven to sear for 10 minutes. Lower heat to 325°F (160°C) and roast it for an additional 15 minutes. Turn the oven off and let the tenderloin rest in the residual heat. After 15 minutes, the roast will be cooked to medium rare.

For more well-done meat, increase the cooking time at the same temperature and use a meat thermometer to determine doneness. Eating rare meat is not recommended by health authorities, particularly for the elderly, the very young, pregnant women or anyone whose immune system may be weakened.

0:30 *To make the potatoes:* Heat the oil in a frying pan over a high heat until it just begins to smoke. Carefully add the potatoes and brown them, stirring occasionally to prevent sticking. When they're nicely browned, pour off any oil remaining in the pan and place it in the oven to keep the potatoes warm. To serve, season them with salt and pepper to taste and garnish with chopped parsley.

0:45 *To prepare chicken livers:* Remove any remaining fibrous tissue, wash the livers and pat them dry. Heat the butter in a frying pan over a high heat, then add the livers and sauté them until they're browned, about 3 minutes. Add the grapes and continue to cook for 2 minutes. Deglaze the pan with white wine, scraping up the bits from the bottom with a wooden spoon, and then let the liquid reduce to a sauce-like consistency. Season it with salt and pepper to taste and serve immediately.

For the main course, cut the beef into ½-inch (1-cm) slices and serve them with the horseradish mustard, potatoes and fresh tomato. When you're ready for the dessert course, wrap the pears in the crepes and serve them with a dollop of sour cream on top.

Sautéed Chicken Livers with White Grapes

7 oz (210 g) livers, trimmed
1 tbsp (15 mL) butter
12 white grapes
¼ cup (50 mL) white wine
Sea salt and fresh pepper

Pepper-Crusted Beef Tenderloin

1 lb (500 g) beef tenderloin, whole
1 clove garlic
5 tbsp (75 mL) horseradish mustard
1 tbsp (15 mL) coarsely ground mixed peppercorns
1 tomato

Parmentier White and Sweet Potatoes

2 medium white potatoes
1 small sweet potato
¼ cup (50 mL) olive oil
Sea salt and fresh pepper
1 tbsp (15 mL) chopped parsley

Pear Crepes

2 red Bartlett pears
1 cup (250 mL) pear nectar
2 premade crepes
2 tbsp (25 mL) sour cream

MENU FOR TWO

Warm Apple and Sausage

Braised Chicken Legs
with Black Beans and Beer

Chocolate Brownies

The ballyhoo and hubbub that is the holiday season, when most cooks take the opportunity to shine and everywhere is fantastic and complicated food, often leaves me yearning for something basic. This menu answers that need while remaining hearty enough to fuel the fires necessary to brave early winter, the holiday season and all the shopping that goes with it.

OF BOOZE AND BROWNIES

> *Madeira should be used when simmering morels, or when a brown sauce requires a nip of sweetness.*

A splash of Madeira adds a pleasing punch to the dynamic duo of apple and sausage, here sautéed with plenty of onions. Madeira is a fortified wine from Portugal, lovely for sipping as an aperitif or dessert wine, but for me its true magic comes to fore when it lends it rich bouquet to foods. A favourite indulgence in the spring is fresh morels lightly simmered in Madeira wine. It's also the wine of choice for introducing a nip of sweetness to a BROWN SAUCE. Combine 1 cup (250 mL) demiglace with 2 tbsp (25 mL) Madeira and 3 tbsp (45 mL) mushroom essence, reduce by a quarter, and you have a sauce of delight and renown.

The braised chicken legs here are adapted from a classic recipe for LAMB SHANKS. First the shanks are seared, then slowly braised in the oven with carrot, onion, beans, tomato and red wine. Oh, and don't forget the garlic. Use plenty of garlic. Braising is a time-honoured method of cooking tough cuts of meats, and after the muscled lamb shank has sat in its warm juices for a couple of hours, it surrenders absolutely.

Slow braising is a marriage dance that unites flavours for a taste at once complex and completely unified. Of course, all this has little to do with cooking in under an hour, but by substituting the smaller and less resistant chicken legs for the lamb shanks, we capture enough of the charm of the original dish.

Christmas is prime time for tinkering elves, happy sugar plum fairies and helpful gnomes of all description. Of course, there are Santa's helpers—where would we be without them? But in Scotland, overworked, stressed-out folk have the benefit of the hard work of brownies to help them through the extra domestic work that comes with the season. While they sleep, the family brownie is said to do all sorts of chores and services for their human companions. They are rough-looking little characters, or so the children say; adults are not able to see most little folk and fairies. Still, if a brownie wants to make the trip across and do my housework while I sleep, well, this would be most welcome. Perhaps I haven't been graced with a beneficent family goblin because they are afraid I might just cook them in a pot. Rest assured, the brownies in this menu are made of chocolate.

CATHERINE'S WINE TIP

Did I say beans and beer don't mix? This dish cries for beer; a delicious Belgian beer called a Lambic or a Chimay. This drink, served cold, has a richness of tone that will counter the garlic and pork in the menu without conflicting with the tomatoes.

0:00 Perhaps it would be most prudent to have a nap and see if a brownie won't just cook this meal for you. If, upon waking, you find your kitchen as cold as when you fell asleep, preheat the oven to 350°F (180°C).

0:01 *To prepare the chicken:* Cut the carrot, onion and celery into ¼-inch (6-mm) diced pieces. Heat the oil in an oven-safe pot over a medium high heat and cook the vegetables until they're soft. Add the chicken legs and brown them on both sides. Deglaze the pot with ⅔ cup (150 mL) beer by scraping up the bits from the bottom with a wooden spoon and add the tomatoes, beans and seasonings. Bring the mixture to a boil, then transfer the pot to hot oven. Cook, uncovered, for 50 minutes or until you're ready for the main course. Additional cooking will only make this dish better. If the sauce is too thin, remove the chicken legs and place the pot over a high heat to reduce. Serve the chicken in the centre of the plate, swimming in the drunken beans.

0:30 *For the brownies:* Melt the chocolate chips and butter by placing them in the hot oven for 1 to 2 minutes. When they're removed from the oven, some of the chips will not be melted, but stirring the mixture with a rubber spatula will allow the residual heat to melt them. Do not leave the chocolate in the oven any longer or it will become grainy. Stir in the sugar, vanilla, egg and Grand Marnier until the mixture is smooth. Gradually stir in the flour and pour into a 5-inch (12.5-cm) greased round cake tin. This is an unusually small pan, so if you do not own one, a mini loaf pan will work as well. Bake the brownies on the middle rack of the oven for 15 to

20 minutes or until they are just set in the middle. I like my brownies to be a little soft and gooey in the centre. To serve, cut into four wedges. Place two on each plate using one to prop the other up and serve with a large scoop of ice cream.

0:50 *To prepare appetizer:* Thinly slice the onion. Heat the oil over a high heat in a regular skillet. Fry the onions until they begin to brown. Peel the apple and cut into ½-inch (1-cm) wedges. Cut the pork into ¼-inch (6-mm) slices. Peel and roughly chop the garlic. Add the apple, pork and garlic to the skillet and fry them until the sausage is browned. Toss or stir constantly to keep onion from burning. Add ¼ cup (50 mL) Madeira to the pan and stir, scraping up the tasty bits from the bottom of the pan. This will reduce very quickly. Serve immediately.

Warm Apple and Sausage

1 medium onion
2 tbsp (25 mL) canola oil
1 apple
1 3- to 4-oz (90- to 120-g) pork sausage
2 cloves garlic
¼ cup (50 mL) Madeira or other fortified wine

Braised Chicken Legs with Black Beans and Beer

2 tbsp (25 mL) canola oil
1 carrot
1 onion
1 stalk celery
2 chicken legs, thighs attached
⅔ cup (150 mL) beer
8 canned plum tomatoes, drained
1 19-oz (540-g) can black beans
2 bay leaves
1 tsp (5 mL) dried chilies
Pinch nutmeg

Chocolate Brownies

⅓ cup (75 mL) semisweet chocolate chips
2 tbsp (25 mL) butter
2 tbsp (25 mL) sugar
1 tsp (5 mL) vanilla
1 egg
1 tsp (5 mL) Grand Marnier
½ cup (125 mL) flour

MENU FOR TWO

Cheese Soup

Cottage Pie

Bread and
Butter Pudding

Comfort is sitting quietly on a tall stool in a warm kitchen, watching the windows steam up on a winter day. Comfort is the memory of your mother's hot soup after a long afternoon of snowball fights or skating at the neighbourhood rink. Comfort is cooking a simple and hearty dish for your family, exactly the way your grandmother taught you. Comfort can mean so many things, but it almost always means food. Because familiarity is crucial to the experience, comfort food is as individual as a person's culture. While one person's solace is a fiery dish of vindaloo, another's may be a generous helping of Caribbean barbecue. I happen to be a fairly typical European mongrel and the English flavours of my comfort foods reflect this heritage.

CHEESE SOUP AND COTTAGE PIE

Cottage pie is much like the humble shepherd's, but is made with beef instead of lamb.

The first course for this cozy dinner for two is a wine-fortified broth enlivened with a liberal dose of cheese. I never prepare this dish in more temperate months, but I have come to think of it as my just reward for braving the bitter cold of each new year. It may be freezing outside, but I have cheese soup and that makes up for everything. A scattering of store-bought croutons makes an acceptable garnish for this dish, but I always have the homemade variety on hand. To make HOMEMADE CROUTONS, cut stale bread into 1-inch (2.5-cm) cubes and toss them in olive oil, herbs, salt and pepper, then spread them out on a baking sheet. Bake 5 to 7 minutes in a 450°F (230°C) oven. These croutons will keep in a sealed container, unrefrigerated, indefinitely. The great thing about making your own croutons, apart from the satisfaction of running a frugal kitchen, is that you can experiment with a variety of tastes. Adding minced garlic to the oil is a personal favourite, although the presence of garlic can trigger bacterial growth, so these croutons should be eaten the same day they are prepared. Try different herb mixes—rosemary croutons go well with lamb soup; oregano and thyme croutons add a satisfying crunch to any salad.

Cottage pie may seem familiar, even if you have never enjoyed it by that name. Shepherd's pie is pretty much the same thing, except that it is traditionally prepared with lamb and cottage pie is made with beef. Whatever the name, the most vital step to preparing a successful pie is mashing the potatoes. The unbearable lightness of beautifully mashed potatoes makes the comfort food, which is why I recently conducted the Great Canadian Mashing Experiment. I prepared three batches of potatoes, using a ricer, a hand masher and a hand mixer. (Never use a food processor or blender unless you have some need for potato glue.)

The ricer makes terrific mashed potatoes; it gives you a smooth, lump-free product but requires a bit of time and effort. The hand mixer is fast, but caution must be exercised: too high a speed or a minute of overwhipping and it is back to the glue factory. The hand masher comes out ahead of the other two, for both texture and speed, taking little more than a minute to produce smooth, light potatoes. Furthermore, with a hand masher, cleanup is a breeze.

Bread and butter puddings enjoy perennial popularity for good reason. First, they are economical—once again we are making use of day-old bread. Second, they are remarkably simple to prepare: Ten minutes to assemble and your pudding is in the oven. Most importantly, bread and butter pudding passes the taste test. You will also love how versatile the basic recipe is. The pudding on this menu features pecans, currants and brandy, but you can easily substitute any flavours you prefer. If you don't fancy the heady taste of brandy-soaked currants, for example, leave them out and make a simple raisin and cinnamon version. One of my favourite variations incorporates a layer of thinly sliced apples at the bottom of the dish and spices the hot milk with rum. As long as you do not alter the ratio of egg, milk, sugar and bread, you can easily create your own version.

The sharp taste of aged cheddar in cheese soup and the savoury flavour of cottage pie will both do best paired with a medium-bodied dry red wine, such as a Côtes du Rhone. Personally, I would forgo wine and match this meal instead with a good English ale. If you are in the mood for a dessert wine, try accompanying the pudding with one of Canada's world-class Late-Harvest Rieslings or Vidals.

0:00 Banish all thoughts of winter and prepare to steam up some windows.

0:01 Preheat oven to 375°F (190°C). Peel the potatoes. Cut each into eight pieces; place them in a pot. Cover with cold salted water and bring it to a boil; cook until the potatoes are soft, about 15 minutes. In a small bowl, soak the currants in brandy.

0:05 Peel the carrot and parsnip; chop into ¼- to ½-inch (6-mm to 1-cm) cubes. In a nonstick skillet over medium high, heat 1 tbsp (15 mL) olive oil; sauté the carrot, parsnip and onion until the onion is soft. Add the beef, breaking up lumps. Cook until the beef begins to brown. Drain the liquid, dust the mixture with 1 tbsp (15 mL) flour and cook 3 to 4 minutes. Stir in the beef stock, tomatoes, peas and savory. Reduce the heat to medium low and simmer gently.

0:30 Drain the potatoes; return them to the heat for a moment to dry. Mash with a hand masher; stir in ¼ cup (50 mL) milk and 2 tbsp (25 mL) butter. Divide the beef mixture between two 1½-cup (375-mL) casserole dishes; cover the tops with mashed potatoes. Place the dishes on a baking sheet in the oven; set the timer for 30 minutes.

0:35 Remove the crusts from challah; spread ½ tsp (2 mL) butter on the bread and use the remaining butter to grease an 8- x 4-inch (1.5-L) loaf pan. Cut the bread into quarters and place them in the dish. Cover with the pecans, currants and brandy. Split the vanilla bean, place it in a saucepan with 1 cup (250 mL) milk; scald the milk by heating it to just below boiling point. (If you're using vanilla extract, add it to the egg yolk and sugar mixture.) Whisk together the egg yolks and sugar until they're light and fluffy. Slowly whisk the hot milk into the yolks; whisk in the cinnamon. Pour the mixture over the bread and set it aside. Create a bain marie by filling a larger baking dish with 1 inch (2.5 cm) hot water. Do not overfill it or the water will overflow the sides when you set your pudding in the baking dish. Set the bain marie dish in the oven to heat it.

0:45 Remove the roots and dark green stems and leaves from the leek. Cut it in half lengthwise and reserve half for another use. Cut the leek into thin slices; rinse them well in a large bowl of cold water; drain. In a large saucepan over medium low, heat 1 tsp (5 mL) olive oil; add 1 tbsp (15 mL) butter. Add the leek and cook until it is soft. Dust the leek with 1 tbsp (15 mL) flour and cook, stirring, for 2 minutes or until the flour begins to brown. Add the white wine and stir until the flour is well incorporated. Pour in the chicken stock and ⅓ cup (75 mL) milk; let simmer 5 minutes. Remove from the heat. Whisk in the parmesan. Serve the soup garnished with grated cheddar and croutons.

0:60 Remove cottage pies from the oven and let them rest until you are ready to serve them. Reduce the heat to 350°F (180°C) and place the bread and butter pudding in the bain marie in the oven. Set the timer for 35 minutes. Serve warm from the oven or at room temperature.

Cheese Soup

1 leek
1 tsp (5 mL) olive oil
1 tbsp (15 mL) butter
1 tbsp (15 mL) all-purpose flour
⅓ cup (75 mL) white wine
1 cup (250 mL) chicken stock
⅓ cup (75 mL) milk or whipping cream
¼ cup (50 mL) grated parmesan
1 oz (30 g) aged white cheddar, grated
2 tbsp (25 mL) croutons

Cottage Pie

2 large Yukon Gold potatoes (about 1 ½ lb/750 g)
1 carrot
1 parsnip
1 tbsp (15 mL) olive oil
¼ cup (50 mL) chopped onion
½ lb (250 g) extra-lean ground beef
1 tbsp (15 mL) all-purpose flour
½ cup (125 mL) beef stock
4 canned plum tomatoes, chopped
¼ cup (50 mL) frozen peas
2 sprigs savory
¼ cup (50 mL) milk
2 tbsp (25 mL) butter

Bread and Butter Pudding

2 tbsp (25 mL) currants
1 tbsp (15 mL) brandy
1 slice (¾-inch/2-cm thick) challah (egg bread)
1 tsp (5 mL) butter, softened
2 tbsp (25 mL) pecan halves
1 vanilla bean or ½ tsp (2 mL) vanilla extract
1 cup (250 mL) milk
2 egg yolks
2 tbsp (25 mL) granulated sugar
¼ tsp (1 mL) ground cinnamon

MENU FOR TWO

Individual Baked Brie

Coq au Vin

Herbed Noodles

Madeleines

We love chicken. Each Canadian consumes more than 50 pounds (25 kg) of chicken annually. With that much *poulet* under our belts, one might think a lingering boredom would set in. Not so. Easy to cook and mild in taste, this adaptable fowl is popular grilled, fried, poached, braised, baked or sautéed.

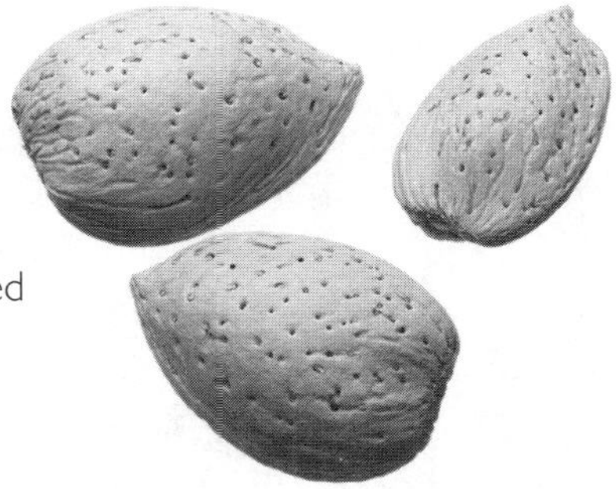

ELEGANT FOWL

Serve this New World Coq au Vin with a Pinot Noir or a Burgundy.

Canadians aren't alone in their love of the bird. Around the world, chicken takes pride of place in curries, fricassees, fajitas and stir-fries. And the first line of defence against cold weather, weary spirits and bodily ills is homemade chicken noodle soup.

Larousse Gastronomique offers more than 50 recipes for classical French treatments of chicken, including coq au vin. Savoury and simple, this dish is enduringly popular. The original recipe was developed to slow-cook a tough old bird until it's tender, but here the cooking time is sped up to accommodate a younger, more supple chicken and a busier schedule. I've also cut down the fat content of the classic recipe.

For the first course, I have created individual baked brie packages. When entertaining a group, you can adapt the recipe to make a BAKED BRIE WHEEL: Slice a whole wheel of brie in half horizontally. Sandwich thinly sliced pears and strawberries between the two discs of cheese. Wrap it up in three sheets of phyllo pastry. Place the package seam side down on a baking sheet, brush it with beaten egg and cover with sliced almonds. Bake at 350°F (180°C) until the almonds and pastry are toasted, 12 to 15 minutes. Like individual baked brie, it should be served immediately. Use low-fat cheese to cut down on calories; the rubbery texture common to some low-fat varieties melts away as the cheese warms up.

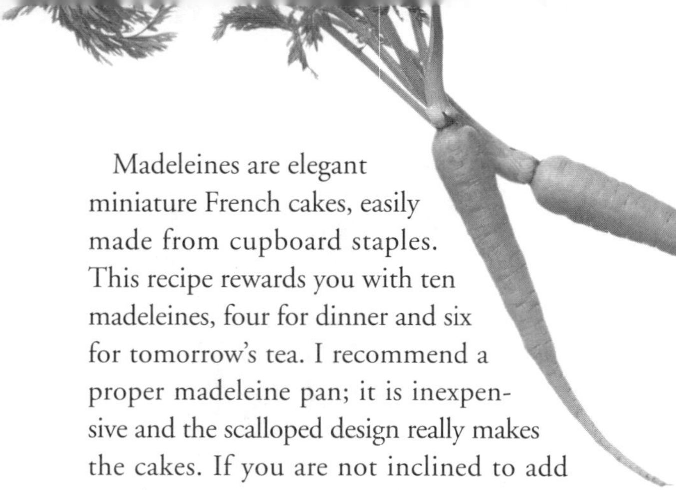

Madeleines are elegant miniature French cakes, easily made from cupboard staples. This recipe rewards you with ten madeleines, four for dinner and six for tomorrow's tea. I recommend a proper madeleine pan; it is inexpensive and the scalloped design really makes the cakes. If you are not inclined to add another pan to your complement, divide the batter among six muffin moulds and increase the baking time from 8 minutes to 12.

A New World Pinot Noir or a red Burgundy is ideal to cook with and to drink with the meal. If you're serving an expensive wine, buy something more economical for cooking.

0:00 *For coq au vin:* With a cleaver, cut each breast crosswise into three pieces. Discard any bone splinters. If you're working ahead, marinate the chicken in ¼ cup (50 mL) red wine, covered, in the refrigerator overnight.

0:01 Boil the water to blanch the onions. Butter the madeleine moulds; set them aside. Place the onions in a bowl and pour the boiling water over top. Drain and cool them under cold water. To peel, cut off the root ends and gently squeeze out the onions. Chop the bacon and fry it in a deep frying pan over medium-high heat. After 2 to 3 minutes, add the onions to pan. Peel the carrot and cut it into ¼-inch (6-mm) cubes; add them to the pan. If the chicken has been marinating, drain and reserve the marinade. Add the chicken to the pan and cook, turning occasionally, until it has browned, 5 to 10 minutes. Meanwhile, quarter the mushrooms and add them to the pan. Cook, stirring occasionally, until the mushrooms are soft, about 5 minutes. Pour off any pools of fat. Add the brandy, stirring to scrape up any bits from the bottom of the pan with a wooden spoon, then add the garlic and thyme. Stir in the flour. Pour in 1½ cups (375 mL) red wine (or 1¼ cups/300 mL red wine plus ¼ cup/50 mL marinade) and bring to boil. Reduce the heat and let it simmer, uncovered, for 30 minutes, turning the chicken occasionally. It does not matter if the chicken cooks longer, but once the sauce is thick enough to coat the back of a spoon, reduce the heat to low. Add up to ¼ cup (50 mL) more wine, if necessary, to prevent further thickening, or remove coq au vin from the heat and cover it to keep it warm. If the sauce is too thin at serving time, remove the chicken from the pan, bring the sauce to a boil and reduce it to the desired consistency. Season to taste with nutmeg, cayenne, salt and pepper just before serving.

0:30 While the chicken is cooking, prepare the madeleines: Preheat the oven to 425°F (220°C). In a bowl, cream together the sugar and butter until they're light and fluffy. Beat in the eggs, vanilla and 2 tsp (10 mL) brandy, if you're using it. In a separate bowl, combine the flour, baking powder and salt. Fold into the wet ingredients. Spoon the batter into the greased madeleine pan and bake on the middle rack for 8 to 10 minutes or until they spring back to the touch. Let them cool slightly, then unmould them. In a small bowl, combine the jam and 1 tsp (5 mL) brandy, if using, and set it aside.

0:45 For the noodles, bring a large pot of salted water to boil over a medium-high heat.

To wrap the brie: Unfurl the phyllo pastry; cut it into two equal squares and brush them with oil. Divide the brie into two wedges and place one on each square. Wrap each piece of cheese in the pastry and place it seam side down on a greased or nonstick baking sheet. Brush the top with egg white. Gently press almonds into the tops. Bake the brie for 3 to 4 minutes on the top oven rack at 425°F (220°C), until the almonds are lightly toasted. Serve immediately with bread.

Between courses, cook the noodles in the boiling water until they're tender but firm to the bite, about 12 minutes. Drain and toss them in parsley and butter. Serve coq au vin over noodles. Garnish with sprigs of thyme.

Just before serving dessert, place two madeleines on each of two serving plates; spread jam over top, then dust with icing sugar.

Individual Baked Brie

1 sheet phyllo, thawed according to package instructions
1 tsp (5 mL) olive oil
3 oz (90 g) low-fat or regular brie
1 egg white
2 tbsp (25 mL) sliced almonds
2 slices baguette or other bread

Coq au Vin

2 skinless chicken breast halves,
bone in (½ to ¾ lb/250 to 375 g each)
10 pearl onions
1 strip bacon
1 carrot
10 small mushrooms
⅓ cup (75 mL) brandy
3 cloves garlic, minced
1 tbsp (15 mL) chopped thyme plus sprigs for garnish
2 tsp (10 mL) all-purpose flour
1½ to 1¾ cups (375 to 425 mL) red wine
(preferably Pinot Noir)
Pinch nutmeg
Pinch cayenne
Sea salt and fresh pepper

Herbed Noodles

2 cups (500 mL) broad egg noodles
2 tbsp (25 mL) chopped parsley
1 tsp (5 mL) butter

Madeleines

⅓ cup (75 mL) granulated sugar
¼ cup (50 mL) butter, softened
2 eggs, at room temperature
½ tsp (2 mL) pure vanilla extract
1 tbsp (15 mL) brandy, optional
⅔ cup (150 mL) all-purpose flour
½ tsp (2 mL) baking powder
Pinch salt
1 tbsp (15 mL) berry jam, such as strawberry
1 tbsp (15 mL) icing sugar

MENU FOR TWO

Steamed Mussels

Cheese Fondue

Mixed Fruit in
Chocolate Sauce

Remember the 1970s? That less-than-inspired period when a hot beef sandwich at the local greasy spoon was considered Canadian Cuisine? Those were the good old, bad old days, when fusion was a thermonuclear reaction and the height of international food chic was the fondue. There was a big old American car in every driveway and a fondue pot in every kitchen. Groovy parties at home weren't complete without the thumping sounds of disco and every guest in the rumpus room was well armed with a cocktail wienie in one hand and a fondue fork in the other. Like bell bottoms, dance music and Burt Bacharach, the fondue is back. It's kitsch, it's retro and the truth is, it's delicious.

SATURDAY NIGHT FONDUE

The fondue is back; it's kitsch, it's retro and the truth is, it's delicious.

There are many versions of this Swiss specialty, but the most familiar and my favourite is the fondue de Valais. Slowly melting gruyère cheese in wine and seasoning it with kirsch (cherry brandy) and a pinch of nutmeg yield a thick and gooey sauce ideal for dipping bread and meat. The addition of cornstarch to even out the texture seems to me a North American adaptation but one with which I wholeheartedly agree. Any fondue I have attempted without it has come out uneven and stringy.

About a million years ago, I met Catherine, the wine consultant for my *Nice Timing* columns, when we both worked at Raclette restaurant in Toronto's fashion district. The restaurant served more than 300 types of wine and several varieties of fondue. Bündnerfleisch, an air-dried beef, was served with the fondue, exactly as Grisons would be served in Switzerland. I have suggested prosciutto as a more readily available alternative, but thinly sliced ham will do as well. It is not traditional to serve vegetables with a cheese fondue, but I do in an attempt to balance out the meal nutritionally.

Mussels are the ideal preamble to this cheesy main course. I find a small portion of a dozen or fewer mussels steamed with garlic, white wine and tomatoes is just enough to dull my hunger sufficiently to avoid an overindulgence of the rich (and fattening) Swiss cheese. When cooking mussels, I seldom set out to market with a recipe in hand. They are the perfect tool to whet your improvisational cooking skills. Equally good steamed in white wine or beer, they can be joined in their pot by nothing more than garlic, or by a combination of black olives, anchovy, thyme and tomato. They can be sautéed with peppers, stuffed with butter or napped with béchamel. Mussels are succulent in soups, perfect for paella and marvellous *à la marinière*. And, if all of this is not enough, they're rich in calcium and iron. Perhaps Popeye was strong to the finish 'cause he ate his spinach, but I'm sure Olive Oyl got her muscles from mussels.

0:00 Since each of these courses needs to prepared à la minute, there is little preparation to be done. It is necessary to spend a few minutes cooking in between courses; however, the benefit to this type of meal is that you can sit down to the appetizer long before the hour is up.

0:01 *For the fondue:* Rub garlic into a small stainless steel pot or fondue pot, then pour in the wine. Grate the cheese. Dissolve the cornstarch in the kirsch. Set all of this near the stove to be assembled just before serving. Cut the bread into 1-inch (2.5-cm) cubes; place them in a basket or bowl and cover to keep fresh. Peel the carrot and cut it into ½-inch (1-cm) cubes. Separate the endive leaves. Arrange the Bündnerfleisch, carrots, tomatoes and endive on two plates.

0:15 *For the fruit salad:* Segment the orange and arrange the pieces with the berries on two plates. Cover them to keep the fruit fresh. Melt the chocolate along with the butter and cream in a stainless steel bowl over hot, not boiling, water, 2 to 3 minutes. Whisk until it's smooth. Set the chocolate aside.

0:30 *To prepare the mussels:* Scrub any dirt from the shells under cold running water and remove the beards. Cultured mussels tend to be very clean. Discard any that are not tightly closed. Chop the onion and mince the garlic. Heat the olive oil in a stainless steel skillet over a medium-high heat. Add the onions and garlic and cook until they're soft. Add the tomatoes and white wine and bring the mixture to a simmer. Add the mussels and thyme and sprinkle with salt and pepper. Cover and steam until all the mussels are fully opened, about 3 to 5 minutes. Do not overcook them or they'll be rubbery. Discard any mussels that have not fully opened.

Serve the mussels immediately in two bowls, with lots of good bread to soak up the juices.

After enjoying the mussels, finish the fondue by placing the pot containing the wine over a high heat until it begins to simmer. Reduce the heat to low and stir in the cheese until it has melted. Stir

CATHERINE'S WINE TIP

One of my favourite wines to suggest with this style of menu at Raclette was a Muscadet sur lie. It's a great wine that connects the mussels with the fondue and should be kept well chilled throughout the dinner.

the nutmeg into the kirsch mixture and continue stirring until the consistency is fairly smooth. Serve immediately in a fondue pot or a small stainless pot over a tea light. When the fondue cools, the texture becomes unpalatable, so it must be kept hot. Serve it with more bread and prepared plates of meat and vegetables and supply fondue or long forks for spearing the food to be dipped in the cheese.

When you're ready for dessert, return the bowl of chocolate to the heat for a moment to warm it, while you halve the banana and cut each half into four wedges. Place them on the plate with the other fruit, drizzle the chocolate sauce over top and serve.

Steamed Mussels

1 lb (500 g) cultured mussels
½ small cooking onion
1 clove garlic
1 tbsp (15 mL) olive oil
¼ cup (50 mL) canned plum tomatoes
¼ cup (50 mL) white wine
4 sprigs thyme
Sea salt and fresh pepper

Cheese Fondue

1 clove garlic
1 cup (250 mL) white wine or Swiss Fendant
8 oz (250 g) gruyère or emmenthal cheese
2 tsp (10 mL) cornstarch
2 tbsp (25 mL) kirsch
¼ loaf good bread
1 carrot
1 head Belgian endive
2 oz (50 g) Bündnerfleisch or prosciutto
6 cherry tomatoes
Pinch nutmeg

Mixed Fruit in Chocolate Sauce

1 clementine orange
2 strawberries (or any berries available)
¼ cup (50 mL) semisweet chocolate chips
1 tbsp (15 mL) butter
¼ cup (50 mL) whipping cream
1 banana

MENU FOR TWO

Corn Bread

Frogmore Stew

Wild Rice Pudding

My great uncle Josephat Duquette was a farmer, working 100 acres outside of Tilbury, Ontario, around the turn of the century. His story appears in my book *Recipes for Homemade Love*, along with the stories of many Canadians, dating from the 1880s onward. The book is a collection of memories and recipes shared by people across the country, and the unifying theme is the love shared within a family and how that love lives on long after the death of a loved one—in many cases for generations. Of course there is food. The recipes cooked by people like Josephat a hundred years ago are still cooked by family members as a way of preserving the past. The wonderful stories people generously shared with me constitute an oral history of the century—not from a grand political or economic viewpoint but through the tender gaze of grandparents and grandchildren. Most of the food is wonderful for its simplicity and I find that I cook out of the book weekly. These recipes date from a time when cupboards stocked only very basic ingredients, and the hard work that was everyone's daily experience left little time to fuss over the family's dinner (sound familiar?). I love that I can always turn to them for something fast and tasty that I usually have the ingredients for.

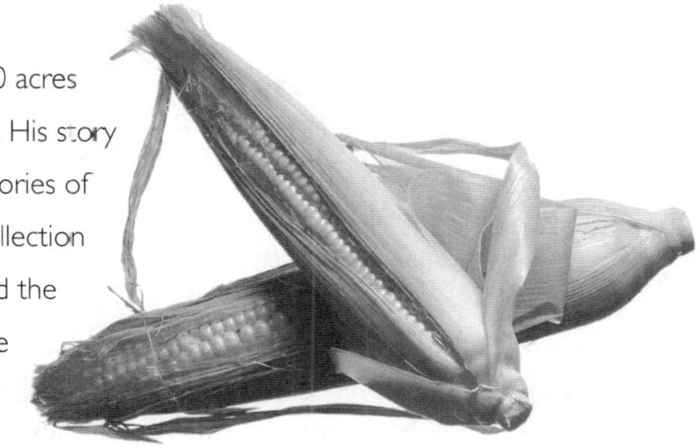

A LOW COUNTRY JAM

Frogmore Stew is a South Carolina Low Country specialty.

Most people baked their own bread and there are several quick breads in the book, ideal for those days when the work of raising the crop, the livestock and seven kids just didn't leave time to bake a yeast bread. Interestingly, there are few days when the work of supporting a family and caring for one child leaves me with time to bake a yeast bread. Still, I love putting a steaming loaf on the table and the corn bread featured in this menu, which takes minutes to assemble before popping it in oven, fits my timetable nicely. Nice timing. I doubt that an Ontario farmer of a hundred years ago would have had South Carolina–styled foods to accompany a simple corn bread, but the world is a much smaller place today. As a fan of good food and interesting people, I celebrate this fact daily.

Working in the professional kitchens of Toronto, both my husband and I have had access to cooks from around the globe. One such talented chef was Kevin Kippers, who worked the cuisine from his native southern United States into the menu at Allen's on the Danforth. Frogmore Stew and Wild Rice Pudding were both introduced to us by Kevin and we've adapted them for this menu. Frogmore Stew is a South Carolina Low Country specialty and the Beaufort County Public Library suggests that it is a relatively new dish. Boiling crab and shrimp along with whatever other vegetables they had on hand was a common practice of the shrimpers in Beaufort County, but the addition of smoked sausage didn't occur until about 40 years ago. I've substituted clams for crab in this winter menu, but when fresh crab is available, I happily add some to the pot.

CATHERINE'S WINE TIP

How about a crisp Vino Verde from the province of Minho near the Spanish border? These wines are fairly low in alcohol content and have a slight, mild carbonation. A refreshing pause from a hearty frogmore stew. With the wild rice pudding I would serve a light, well-chilled Prosecco from the Veneto region of Italy. This wine is just a little sweet and adds a gentle finish to a filling dinner.

0:00 Low Country food calls for Low Country Blues like the music of South Carolina's own Blues Doctor, Mr. Drink Small. If your blues collection doesn't include more obscure artists, go with who you love.

0:01 Preheat oven to 450°F (230°C). Combine the milk and vinegar and let them stand until the milk curdles, about 10 minutes. Cook the rice for the pudding by placing it in 2½ cups (625 mL) cold water. Bring it to a boil, then let it simmer until the kernels pop, about 45 minutes.

0:10 Continue making the corn bread: Blend the flour, cornmeal, baking soda and salt together. Whisk in the milk mixture, and then the eggs and butter. Mix until it just comes together. Pour it into a greased 1-quart (1-L) bread pan and bake it on the middle rack of the oven for 20 to 25 minutes or until the bread comes away from the side of the pan. Serve slathered with butter or goat cheese.

0:25 *For the frogmore stew:* Heat the oil in a medium-sized pot over a high heat. Cube the onion, carrot, celery and sweet potato and slice the sausage into ½-inch (1-cm) pieces. Sauté all along with the new potatoes for 5 minutes, stirring often to prevent burning. Cover with stock and bring it to boil. Reduce the heat to a high simmer, add the thyme and bay leaf, and let cook for 10 minutes. Cut

the corn into ½-inch (1-cm) coins. Wash the clams under cold running water and discard any that are not tightly closed. Add the corn and clams to the stew, cover and cook until the clams open, about 8 to 10 minutes. Discard any clams that do not open. Check the potatoes for doneness and continue to simmer until they're soft. Keep the stew warm over a low heat until you're ready to serve it, then increase the temperature to simmer, add the shrimp and cook until they're pink on the outside and white on the inside, about 3 minutes. Serve immediately.

0:45 When the rice is cooked, finish the dessert: Add vanilla to the whipping cream and scald the mixture by bringing it just to the boiling point over a medium-high heat; then remove it from the heat. While the cream is heating, whisk the sugar into the yolks until they're pale and ribbony. Slowly whisk the hot milk into the eggs until they're mixed together. Drain the rice and add it to the custard mixture; stir in the vanilla. Return the pot to a low heat and cook, stirring constantly, until the liquid begins to thicken. Transfer the pudding to two dessert bowls and refrigerate until you're ready to serve it.

Corn Bread

1 cup (250 mL) milk
2 tbsp (25 mL) vinegar
1 cup (250 mL) flour
1 cup (250 mL) cornmeal
1 tsp (5 mL) baking soda
1 tsp (5 mL) salt
2 eggs, beaten
2 tbsp (25 mL) melted butter
Butter or goat cheese

Frogmore Stew

1 tbsp (15 mL) olive oil
½ onion
1 carrot
1 stalk celery
¼ sweet potato
5 oz (140 g) smoked sausage
4 new potatoes
2 cups (500 mL) chicken stock
4 sprigs thyme
1 bay leaf
1 cob corn
6 clams in shell
6 large shrimp

Wild Rice Pudding

4 tbsp (60 mL) wild rice
1 vanilla bean, split
¾ cup (175 mL) whipping cream
2 egg yolks
2 tbsp (25 mL) sugar

Notes

Notes

Index

T

Z